Praise for *Zero Time*

"The authors crystallize a complete new vision for customer interaction based on alignment and communities. At last, the customer is at the core of the innovation process. Such a (re)discovery of customer value is certain is to have impact on the bottom-line as well as open doors to new markets—the cornerstone of success in the emerging economy."

—Debra M. Amidon, CEO of ENTOVATION International Ltd. and author, *Innovation Strategy for the Knowledge Economy*

"*Zero Time,* addresses the issues that time has introduced into the delivery of customer satisfaction in an era in which time is of the essence in customer satisfaction. It addresses the effort to close all gaps that interfere with providing customer satisfaction. It provides a series of well-chosen examples about how successful industries have closed those gaps and provided maximum service to customers. Reading it will be well worth the time."

—Robert M. Berdahl, Chancellor, University of California, Berkeley

"If time is money, *Zero Time* is worth Zillions. . . . An executive's must-read on one of the hottest topics of our time. . . . A book of timeless value."

—Dr. Jim Botkin, President, InterClass International Corporate Learning Association

"This book should be required reading for every CEO."

—Don Carty, Chairman, President, and CEO, American Airlines, Inc.

"Like me, you probably use the phrase Internet time to convey the notion of speed to decision and action and as a measure of how things work (or should work) in the new economy. After you read this important book, you'll understand that there's something much more profound than high speed at work in the economy today and, even more so, tomorrow. I highly recommend *Zero Time* to all who seek success in the new economy and to those who just want to understand what's going on."

—Jared L. Cohon, President, Carnegie Mellon University

"The relativity theory had discovered the importance of time for mechanics. George Kozmetsky and his co-authors emphasize the new time dimension of business. *Zero Time* is a book full of vision but also of very practical examples of companies who have adjusted to the new need for instant customer satisfaction."

—Bertrand Collomb, President, LAFARGE

"The fascinating philosophy of *Zero Time* will prove to be crucial for companies to succeed in the Internet age. I found this book to be most thought-provoking and innovative and believe that it will have enormous impact on conventional thinking on a global level. . . . With this publication, the authors continue to make significant contributions to the world of business, and we are deeply grateful for their remarkable insight and vision."

—William H. Cunningham, Chancellor, The University of Texas System

"Drawing upon their experience, deep insights, and illuminating illustrations, the authors have written an excellent and highly original work on how companies can effectively combine motivated individuals, empowering processes, and internet-centered technology to provide instant, reliable, and consistent customer value.

"This book contains some of the most powerful and creative ways of thinking about learning systems, customer focus and delight, trusting corporate cultures, and organizational agility that I have ever seen, all presented in an interesting and logical fashion."

>—David M. Darst, Managing Director, Morgan Stanley Dean Witter, and
>author of *The Complete Bond Book* and *The Handbook of the Bond
>and Money Markets*

"Combining anecdote, case histories, insight and imagination, *Zero Time* builds on ideas of empowerment and customer focus to show how the opportunities created by the digital age can enhance business performance."

>—Professor Sandra Duncan, Director of the Judge Institute and Master of
>Sidney Sussex University of Cambridge, England

"*Zero Time* is a must read for any CEO who expects to successfully navigate the New Economy. Drs. Yeh, Kozmetsky, and Pearlson provide not only the nautical charts necessary for this journey, but a revolutionary set of Ten Commandments which businesses must follow to thrive in the new millennium."

>—Paul Hirschbiel, President, Eden Capital

"*Zero Time* is a thought-provoking treatise. The concepts presented will prove applicable to all sectors of the business world. Medicine, still a cottage industry, representing approximately 14 percent of the GNP, will be reshaped in accordance with the principles expressed."

>—Stephen H. Hochschuler, M.D., Founder, Texas Back Institute

"A must read book for the CEO who will lead his/her company to success in the twenty-first century."

>—Adm. (retired) Bob R. Inman

"This is not a book of the Present Time, but a book of Future Time full of willingness. By learning the philosophy of *Zero Time,* we will be able to create every opportunity for Futurity brought about by the Digital Revolution."

>—Fumio Itoh, Dean, Graduate School of International Politics, Economics
>and Business, Aoyama Gakuin University

"*Zero Time* will become a secular bible for the twenty-first century—speed in closing the gaps is essential, not only for success but for survival."

>—Herbert D. Kelleher, Chairman, President, and CEO,
>Southwest Airlines Co.

"This book is a rare and wonderful combination—a lively, readable work that provides a research-based analysis of what distinguishes true world class companies from the rest of the pack. This path-breaking book on the real lessons of the New Economy and modern management should be required reading for business and workforce leaders, investors, and all concerned with regional economies."

>—Jamie Kenworthy, Executive Director, Alaska Science and Technology
>Foundation

"The authors characterize five factors critical to successful business ventures in today's competitive environment. Like the mathematicians of old, they have discovered the concept of zero, and elevated it to a position of primacy for transaction time, learning timeframes, value gaps and the like. Fast-paced and laced with cogent examples, the book conveys a sense of the intensity that pervades modern business practice. Conceptually novel and efficiently informative."

> —Alvin L. Kwiram, Vice Provost for Research,
> University of Washington

"The authors of this book are both erudite and practical. They have produced a work of lasting value for anyone interested in how business institutions work."

> —Hans Mark, Director of Defense Research and Engineering

"*Zero Time* is a decade ahead of its time and the competition."

> —Edward A. Miller

"*Zero Time* boldly identifies the point at which the much-noticed innovations of companies as different as Fedex, Dell Computer, General Electric, and Cisco will converge as a dramatically new model for American business. Many have seen fleeting glimpses of this future from different perspectives; here is a book that finally sees the startling new corporate reality as a whole. From the pile of new volumes on corporate change, this is the one to select for your strongest essential insight."

> —Barry Munitz, President and CEO, The J. Paul Getty Trust

"*Zero Time* makes fascinating reading. It is a precious guide to the successful stories of the major U.S. companies viewed from an original point of view. In the past, traditional economics tried to follow pluriannual programs. This is no more so in our information society. As the author explains, we try to reach zero time companies. This is a goal which some companies are steadily approaching. A lucid introduction to recent aspects of economics."

> —Ilya Prigogine, Director of the International Solvay Institutes for
> Physics and Chemistry, Brussels, Belgium; Director of the Ilya
> Prigogine Center for Studies in Statistical Mechanics, Thermodynamics
> and Complex Systems, University of Texas at Austin, Nobel Prize
> winner

"It is a marvelous piece of modern management advice and guidance. One can almost believe in the concepts and become a fan and promoter of *Zero Time,* because the complex discussion of their existence and use are so appended with modern, live examples of their value in the world community of great corporations that they are ALIVE."

> —Dr. George A. Roberts

"Like *In Search of Excellence, Zero Time* shatters the old paradigm. It's a new way of thinking and executing that will provoke controversy, and ultimately, enlightenment."

> —Dr. Robert Ronstadt, Director, IC² Institute, The University of Texas
> at Austin

"Zero Time is the executive's guide to the new millennium! Yeh, Kozmetsky, and Pearlson have distilled the essence of the chaotic dynamics of today's paradigm-busting business world into a coherent set of principles and guidelines for success. Rather than offering an abstract theory, they provide a wealth of case studies that not only illustrate their thesis, but can serve as models for emulation or adaptation as well. This book should be a 'must read' for CEO's and CIO's alike if they want their companies to be among the survivors in the new economy."

—Alan B. Salisbury, Ph.D., Past President, Learning Tree International

"Zero Time delivers an outstanding analysis of the Electronic Business generation and how corporations must adapt to Internet speed."

—Ralph J. Szygenda, Group Vice President and CIO,
General Motors Corporation

"Reading this book will strongly motivate you to focus on the fundamentals of your business and think 'out of the box' to make breakthrough operating changes."

—Professor Jack Thorne, David T. and Lindsay J. Morgenthaler, Professor of Entrepreneurship, Graduate School of Industrial Administration, and Director of the Donald H. Jones Center for Entrepreneurship, Carnegie Mellon University

"Zero Time analyzes the complexity of today's competitive E-business and provides a blueprint for developing a cutting edge strategy for your organization."

—Fran Ulmer, Lieutenant Governor, State of Alaska

"Zero Time breaks important new ground. The Zero Time concept will significantly impact management thinking as we begin the new millennium. Drs. Yeh, Kozmetsky, and Pearlson are about to join the ranks of Tom Peters, Michael Porter, and Andy Grove."

—Robert E. Witt, President, The University of Texas at Arlington

"Zero Time provides powerful insights into corporate best practice, while at the same time laying out principles that can improve the performance of any organization."

—John Yochelson, President, Council on Competitiveness

Zero Time™

Providing Instant Customer Value—Every Time, All the Time

Raymond Yeh
Keri Pearlson
George Kozmetsky

John Wiley & Sons, Inc.

New York • Chichester • Weinheim • Brisbane • Singapore • Toronto

To Helen, Priscilla, Elaine, and Stephanie. Their love and support have helped me to be who I am today.

R.Y.

To Yale, Hana, Ben, and Shirley. They enrich my life in ways words cannot express.

K.P.

To Ronya, Greg, Nadya, Cindy, Aaron, Bethany, Daniel, Jordan, Sarah, Taylor, Caitlin, Tracey, and Jack. Their love and support have helped make me what I am.

G.K.

Zero Time is a trademark of Raymond Yeh.

This book is printed on acid-free paper. ∞

Copyright © 2000 by Raymond Yeh, Keri Pearlson, and George Kozmetsky. All rights reserved.

Published by John Wiley & Sons, Inc.
Published simultaneously in Canada.

This publication is designed to provide accurate and authoritative information in regard to the subject matter covered. It is sold with the understanding that the publisher is not engaged in rendering professional services. If professional advice or other expert assistance is required, the services of a competent professional person should be sought.

ISBN 0-471-39245-0

Printed in the United States of America.

10 9 8 7 6 5 4 3 2 1

FOREWORD

AS THE WORLD CHANGES FRANTICALLY AROUND US, MANAGERS are often at a loss as what to do. It is easy to resort to the old trusted model of trying to be more efficient and of working harder. It seems that we are constantly in a state of "dizzying disorientation brought on by the premature arrival of the future," as predicted by Alvin Toffler in *Future Shock*. Indeed, in the fiercely competitive environment of the twenty-first-century digital economy, industries no longer matter as your competitors come out of nowhere and everywhere. What does matter is a leader's ability to anticipate, sense, and respond as they gear their firms for the future.

At Dell Computer Corporation, for example, it's not about how much inventory we have, but how fast it's moving through the cycle. Velocity, or the rate at which our business processes happen, becomes a crucial measure for us. As we compete in fast-changing and unpredictable markets, our focus on velocity helps us create the order and discipline needed to purposefully spark innovation within the desired time frame. As our velocity increases, the volume of our business increases with it. The ultimate result of our undivided attention to velocity is increased value to our stakeholders: customers, partners, shareholders, and employees.

One of the most challenging problems for hypergrowth companies like Dell is the ability to manage the conflict between empowerment and alignment. While leaders must empower their employees to gain velocity, they must also make sure that each empowered unit drives toward the same goal. Zero Time thinking epitomizes the ideal of our focus on velocity; namely, a friction-free organization in which each individual or unit is moving at blazing speed, and all are instinctively aligned. The five disciplines of Zero Time proposed by the authors represents a revolutionary new philosophy of leadership for creating a friction-free global organization. What amazes me about these disciplines is their simplicity and practicality.

Zero Time, in my opinion, is the future blueprint for all twenty-first-century organizations. Leaders must practice Zero Time thinking as a way to sharpen their own processes for anticipating the future and preparing for emerging opportunities.

This book is a captivating read, and the authors consistently illustrate their concepts with real examples. Their concepts are a natural next step in the evolution of management practices, and the impact will be revolutionary. This is a well-written book that uses plain language to convey practical, well thought-out ideas. I highly recommend this book to anyone with the management responsibility to guide his or her company to leadership in the new economy.

Tom Meredith
CFO, Dell Computer Corporation

ACKNOWLEDGMENTS

WE ARE GREATLY INDEBTED TO MANY INDIVIDUALS WHO HELPED make this book a reality. We have received invaluable advice from a number of people who have read drafts of the chapters and given us ideas to make them stronger. We want to specifically thank Linda Bailey, John Coné, Max Hung, Nancy Lee Hutchins, Con Kenney, Nick Morgan, Ben Ostrofsky, Charlie Rees, Nancy Richey, Rafael Sagalyn, Jordan Scott, Ralph Szygenda, Scott Van Valkenburg, and Randy Yeh. We also greatly appreciated the help we received from Gina Imperato and her colleagues at *Fast Company* magazine. We spoke with dozens of managers and executives who gave us stories from their experiences, and we thank them.

We are grateful to IC² and the University of Texas at Austin for their support of this work. Robert Ronstadt, Dave Gibson, and Barbara Fossum, in particular, were very helpful in providing us a place to work, and an environment in which our ideas have germinated. Partial funding for writing this book was received from the NSF AAMRC project, and we thank them for their support. Students in Dr. Pearlson's Managing Systems classes in the Information Management Program at the Graduate School of Business at UT provided early feedback and comments on our concepts; thank you.

As with any work of this magnitude, we could not have done it without unfailing support of our editors and assistants. We particularly thank Marcus Pizzola, a graduate student who did some early research for us and who was involved in our early discussions of the disciplines; Stephanie Yeh, who edited all of our separate drafts and rephrased everything in our "common voice" on an incredibly tight schedule; Pattie Roe, George's assistant, who helped us find the time we needed to collaborate and get the job done; and Renana Meyer and Jeanne Glasser, our fabulous editors at John Wiley & Sons who managed the project through the minefield of publishing for us. It was their energy every time we spoke with them that gave us confidence this project would soon be a book we could be proud of.

One other group of people must be mentioned: our spouses and families. We individually and collectively thank them, Priscilla and Stephanie Yeh, Ronya Kozmetsky, Yale and Hana Pearlson. Each of us understands the sacrifices each of you made so we could write *Zero Time*. We love you.

In the end, we are very proud of this book and of the ideas included in it. Thank you to all of those who helped make it possible.

R.Y.

K.P.

G.K.

CONTENTS

INTRODUCTION

See Differently, Act Instantly!

E-businesses are taking business away from traditional brick-and-mortar-based enterprises. The hot competition between amazon.com and Barnes&Noble.com has the business world abuzz with speculation. Barnes & Noble saw its margins begin to erode when amazon.com emerged as the online bookstore powerhouse. As a follower to the digital market, Barnes & Noble had to shift into high gear to get online in an attempt to win back market share. The same scenario is now being played out in almost every industry, including music, news, toys, cosmetics, pharmaceuticals, auctions, and financial services. It's happening in both business-to-business and business-to-consumer transactions. If it hasn't happened yet in your industry, it will.

If it hasn't happened in your industry yet, it will.

The digital rat race is off to a fast start. And winning this race is not about outrunning the competition. It's about not having to run at all. How? By seeing the world from a different perspective, where the seemingly impossible becomes obvious. It's all about time—Zero Time.

In Zero Time, you can fulfill your customers' needs instantly. In a Zero Time organization, every business process is instantly executed in response to customer needs; learning occurs automatically as needed; managers and employees have the knowledge and ability to make decisions instantly; and suppliers provide needed parts and services immediately. In short, Zero Time means that your organization acts and responds instantly to market changes.

Many companies already seem capable of responding instantly. For example, Disney resorts and Ritz-Carlton hotels are known for their outstanding service, which can be customized specifically to their guests' individual needs, seemingly at a moment's notice. These companies are able to offer such service by constantly monitoring their customers' requests, then immediately converting them into services valued by the customer. Similarly, Progressive Insurance earns customer loyalty with its instant settlement policy, whereby Progressive agents are authorized to immediately offer customers a settlement check at the scene of the accident. On the other side of the world, Singapore's Economic Development Board (EDB) played a crucial role in transforming the small city-state of Singapore from a third world country into a global financial mecca in less than 30 years. EDB achieved this success by supplying multinational corporations, Singapore's primary customers, with instant and comprehensive business support. All these organizations consistently outpace their competitors because they see things differently, in Zero Time, the driver behind their successful business strategies.

Zero Time means being able to fulfill your
customers' needs instantly.

In the past several decades, companies such as Wal-Mart, FedEx, Dell Computer Corporation, and Cisco Systems have been growing at astounding rates by offering customers instant response. These companies are focused on time. In the book *Competing Against Time,* authors G. Stalk and T. Hout found that time-based companies like these were able to respond to customers at least 60 percent faster, grow 3 to 4 times faster, and have at least double the profit advantage over their nearest competitors.[1] These elite companies recognize the importance of time as a key competitive advantage in the digital age.

Time is at the core of the digital business world. Successful companies understand how the time imperative can translate into market opportunities. FedEx knows that its customers will pay a premium to ensure that their deliveries arrive on time. Progressive Insurance understands that its customers value its instant settlement policy. Dell recognizes the advantage of a "build to order" manufacturing process that guarantees product delivery within five days of placing the order. Intel and 3M, among others, see the value of "time pacing"[2] whereby product lines are turned over very quickly to keep pace with developing technology and customer expectations.

Elite companies understand how the time
imperative can translate into market opportunities.

Of course, a Zero Time company requires Zero Time managers who understand that total customer satisfaction and instant fulfillment are the keys to success. For instance, Michael Dell, CEO of Dell Computer Corporation, saw the advantage of offering custom-built computer systems directly to customers, while Compaq and IBM were still concentrating on distributing their computers through retailers and dealers. FedEx is another company that has succeeded by focusing on instant customer service. Laurie Tucker, senior vice president at FedEx, focuses on "how to design a compelling customer experience" that is instantly fulfilling. Says Tucker, "This company has always listened to the customer. Now it's about anticipating the customer." She adds, "Our customers are moving at Internet speed, so they need us to respond at Internet speed."[3] From middle managers to CEOs, these leaders have guided their companies to great success by using aspects of the Zero Time approach to combine customer intimacy with instant fulfillment.

Zero Time companies, guided by Zero Time managers, move with speed, instinctively. They are able to respond instantly to ever changing customer demands and the volatile business terrain. Research conducted at dozens of evolving Zero Time organizations reveals that not only can these organizations compete well in existing markets, they also create and dominate new markets.

I See, Therefore I Act

Zero Time companies see and respond to new opportunities differently from their competitors. The competition between Hewlett-Packard (HP) and Kodak in the camera and film industry illustrates how a company thinking in Zero Time can tackle and defeat an established market leader. While other competitors might think only of trying to outperform Kodak, the market leader, HP saw a different opportunity. HP predicted the convergence of digital technology with photography and responded with an aggressive strategy. Today, with its licensed digital camera, HP enables users to edit digital images on their PCs, then send them anywhere via the Internet, instantly. The recipient can just as quickly print the pictures with their HP printers, skipping the entire film development process. By eliminating both the use of film and the need for film development—Kodak's bread and butter—HP's products and services have redefined a marketplace once dominated by

Kodak. While Kodak is trying to catch up by creating kiosks at its distribution channels, providing a free "picture CD" with each roll of processed film, and by forming an alliance with America Online (AOL), HP's new vision and aggressive Zero Time response has already disrupted Kodak's prior market power.

In Zero Time, ideas are acts.

Furthermore, the Zero Time perspective enables businesses to reach outstanding levels of performance without the chaotic disruption brought about by traditional approaches such as restructuring and reengineering. We have seen this type of forward thinking before, with the zero defects concept. Designing for zero defects is different from simply improving quality; it means rethinking the entire production line to ensure that no defects are made at any station along the way. Incremental improvements, on the other hand, are aimed at *containing* defects within certain predetermined levels, with the goal of eventually reaching zero defects. By thinking incrementally, organizations may never reach the zero defects standard, since this mentality may block out the more innovative thought processes required to achieve the goal. In contrast, companies that practice zero defects have rethought their entire production process.

Just as the zero defects movement is not just about achieving incremental quality improvement, Zero Time is not just about reducing cycle time. It's about creating and implementing innovative solutions to achieve instant fulfillment. Consider the difference between Zero Time and real time. In a review of James Gleick's book *Faster,* journalist Gina Imperato posed the question: "What is real time?" Imperato quotes Gleick: "Real-time scheduling, real-time cataloging . . . all these mean a tiny bit more than just fast or not too late. Whatever real time is, we want it."[4] In other words, real time is about increasing the pace of business. But speed itself is no guarantee of success, which is why Zero Time is about achieving the standard of delivering instant and total customer gratification.

In the new digital competition, just being
faster is not enough.

With Zero Time, we start with the goal of delivering total fulfillment *instantly*. In the same way, companies that seek to be Zero Time organizations must approach their businesses with a fresh perspective that eschews the traditional management models and process methods. Zero Time companies and their managers need to *see* differently so that they can discover hidden markets, then create new products and services that serve the customers in these markets. They may even need to create new industries, since acting in Zero Time means moving instantly to be the first to recognize and dominate emerging markets. Companies in both the high- and low-technology industries, such as Cisco, Dell, and Wal-Mart capitalize on this approach, and thus have become the leaders and trendsetters in their respective industries.

"I see, therefore I act" embodies the philosophy of Zero Time. As soon as a need is recognized, it is met. In other words, ideas are acts. In the new digital competition, just being faster is not enough. To win, we must see differently and act instantly. We must operate in Zero Time.

Crossing the Chasm

ALMOST FIVE GENERATIONS AGO, HENRY FORD IMAGINED THE FU-
ture democratization of the automobile. He wanted "to build
a motor car for the great multitudes" by making it affordable
for everyone. He imagined that "the horse will have disap-
peared from our highways, the automobile will be taken for
granted."[1] Then he proceeded to turn that image into reality.
With the invention of the assembly line, Ford became the
undisputed leader in the automobile industry.

The new e-business infrastructure has shaken up
the value chain in new and unpredictable ways.

In more recent times, when GE chairman Jack Welch assumed the reins of power, he decisively changed the company
focus from manufacturing industry and instead began creating

1

lean, high-performing divisions oriented to the service industry. He took this aggressive action despite GE's extraordinarily positive cash flow and public standing because he saw that the service industry would quickly outstrip manufacturing, making it necessary to reposition the company for the future. Today, GE's assets and market value stand at nearly $300 billion, with more than $90 billion in sales, while the number of employees has decreased from 440,000 to 260,000, evidence of the company's vital productivity. John Chambers, too, saw a different future for his company. When he took the reins at Cisco Systems, he had a clear vision of the infrastructure for new business, e-business. First he identified how his company could make this vision a reality, then he formed strategic partnerships to complement Cisco's internal capabilities. In this way, Chambers was able to turn Cisco into a dominating force in the networking equipment marketplace. Likewise, Steve Case led AOL into the leadership position in the networking services industry, outmaneuvering earlier leaders such as CompuServe and Prodigy. Case's vision was to provide a portal, and content, on the Internet using a simple, ubiquitous format. Customers today are able to quickly and easily access proprietary AOL services as well as any Internet services they desire. AOL became the benchmark for all other competitors in this arena.

[These visionaries] contradicted the prevailing business wisdom of their time, and actively prepared their companies for the future.

All of these Zero Time leaders not only saw a different vision from their peers, but they often contradicted the prevailing business wisdom of their time, and actively prepared their companies to intercept their envisioned future marketplace.

They seemed to know instinctively how to steer their companies down counterintuitive paths to reach global market domination, not just success. They took risks and made decisions that were seemingly incomprehensible to their competitors. In short, they saw differently, and acted instantly.

Zero Time managers will take seemingly unusual, outrageous, or strange actions because they will see differently and act instantly.

The value of Zero Time leaders being willing to act on what they see is incalculable. Consider Wal-Mart. Founder Sam Walton built an insurmountable advantage by selling to the emerging markets in small towns, markets of which Sears Roebuck, the leading retailer of the 1960s and 1970s, was totally unaware. By serving the markets in smaller towns, previously considered inconsequential by the market leaders, Wal-Mart leapfrogged over virtually all of its competitors, and in the process revolutionized the industry by introducing a completely different business model. Similarly, Herb Kelleher at Southwest Airlines built his company into the most profitable airline by circumventing the traditional business model. Zero Time managers are not afraid to look into the dark corners and perhaps even strange places to find new opportunities. More important, they are prepared to risk the futures of their companies to pursue what they find there.

The Chasm: Providing Instant CUSTOMERization

A great chasm separates companies guided by Zero Time leaders from their competitors—a chasm that, if crossed, can yield market leadership, even market dominance. This chasm represents a company's capability to totally and instantly meet its customers' needs.

Being able to completely respond to customer needs in this fashion is called *CUSTOMERization*. A Zero Time company achieves CUSTOMERization by continuously transforming detailed knowledge of the customer into high-value products and services. To cross the chasm, a company must combine CUSTOMERization with instant response to customers. In short:

$$\text{Zero Time} = \text{CUSTOMERization} + \text{Instant Action}$$

To be able to act instantly, Zero Time companies must eliminate the organizational resistance caused by the breakdown of its relationships with these entities:

- Customers.
- Employees.
- Processes.
- Knowledge.
- Supply chain partners.

Further, the breakdown of the interactions between these entities only widens the chasm.

Crossing the Chasm

To become a Zero Time organization, a traditional enterprise must cross this chasm. Each breakdown creates lag time, or the gap between a needed action and its actual execution. This automatically causes communication problems and delays. Delay in acting in any of these five key managerial areas of business operations, depicted by the circles in Figure 1.1, prevents organizations from responding instantly to customer needs. The figure illustrates the five gaps within traditional

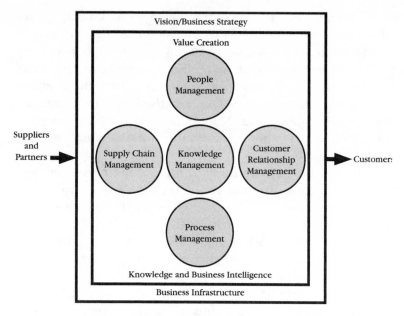

Figure 1.1 Elements of today's business.

organizations, as well as the four boundary conditions, which are vision and business strategy, value creation, knowledge and business intelligence gathering, and business infrastructure. To operate in Zero Time, companies must close these five gaps.

> To achieve instant action, Zero Time companies must eliminate the organizational resistance.

Because the explosion of e-business has so severely disrupted both the global business structure and the business strategy and value creation processes, the traditional management approaches—supply chain management, knowledge management, customer relationship management, people management, and process management—though necessary are no longer sufficient to create competitive advantage. Consequently, companies are scrambling to rethink everything from their business strategy to the way they gather and use business intelligence. More important, they are forced to consider the way they create value for the customer and other stakeholders.

In the traditional twentieth-century value chain concept, value is gradually accumulated along the value chain, reaching its peak when products or services are finally delivered to the customer. In today's virtual marketplace, value can be immediately created at beginning of the chain, in the form of information, which can be readily packaged and delivered. For example, prior to the delivery of a package, FedEx customers can track its progress via the company's online tracking system. That capability is very valuable to the FedEx customers. Thus, FedEx creates value for its customers both with tracking information and guaranteed package delivery. Moreover, expanding the traditional value chain, which flows linearly from supplier to customer, the new virtual value chain delivers value to suppliers as well as customers. For instance, as customers order computers from Dell's online system, market trend data is sent to Dell's suppliers, such as Intel, in near Zero Time, thereby creating value for suppliers in the form of reliable forecasting data.

The new e-business infrastructure is forcing every company to rethink the way it does business, including finding methods to compete effectively in with both physical and virtual marketplaces. But many companies are floundering as they wade through a sea of management fads, unsure of which to follow. To their rescue is the Zero Time approach, which offers a comprehensive way of bridging the five management gaps, enabling companies to deliver instant CUSTOMERization, as shown in Figure 1.2.

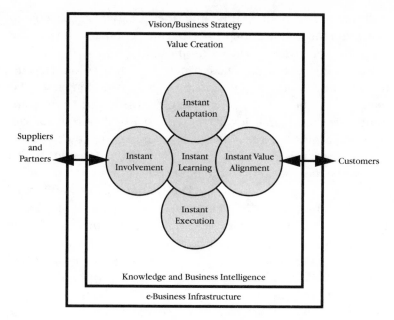

Figure 1.2 Crossing the chasm through five Zero Time disciplines.

Five Zero Time disciplines bridge these gaps:

- Instant Value Alignment.
- Instant Learning.
- Instant Adaptation.
- Instant Execution.
- Instant Involvement.

We introduce these disciplines briefly here, then present a full discussion in the following chapters.

Instant Value Alignment

Customers want instant gratification. They want it "free, perfect, and now," as Marshall Industries CEO Robert Rodin describes in his book of the same title.[2] Customer relationship management is not enough. Zero Time companies need the discipline of *Instant Value Alignment.*

Zero Time companies take a new perspective on the customer. They understand that market share is no longer a valid measure of success. In today's digital world, customers are more fickle, and their loyalty is won or lost on *each* transaction. Regardless of the current size of a company's market share, customers can easily be lured away by more clever and responsive competitors in the next transaction.

Instant Value Alignment dictates that companies no longer pursue market share by trying to satisfy every single customer. Rather, they select a specific group of "right" customers, and deliver absolute gratification by aligning their values with customer values, thereby locking in customer loyalty for life. We call this *customer share.* Customer share is a much more meaningful measure than market share because it provides lifetime business for the company.

Customer share is a more meaningful measure
of success than market share.

Having selected their right customers, Zero Time companies develop the core competencies that enable them to custom-fit their product or services to each of their customers. That means developing a deep understanding of the customer, then proceeding to delight the customer. To achieve Instant Value Alignment means not only understanding the needs of the immediate customer, but the needs of the customer's customer as well. For instance, Honda's goal is to deliver automobiles that not only sell well for its direct customers, the distributors of Honda products, but that also satisfy the ultimate customer, the driver. To that end, Honda carefully aligns its values with the values of the drivers by matching the age of design team members with that of targeted drivers.

Mastery of the Instant Value Alignment discipline enables companies to anticipate changes in customer needs, and shift their products and services to meet those needs. To do this requires that companies know their customers intimately, and actively engage them in the design process so that their needs are anticipated far in advance. For example, Cisco Systems has formalized a process by which customer feedback is incorporated into the design of its products and services. This practice, implemented early in the company's history, keeps Cisco aligned with customer values, and remains part of its core strategy. Figure 1.3 summarizes the essence of the Instant Value Alignment discipline.

Instant Learning

For Zero Time companies, learning is a natural part of work, not separate from work. Zero Time companies educate employees while they work, as the need arises. They practice the discipline of *Instant Learning*. This discipline helps

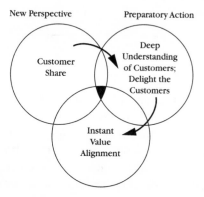

Figure 1.3 Essence of the Instant Value Alignment discipline.

companies to train workers in ways that enhance, rather than interfere with, the organization's productivity.

The Instant Learning discipline requires a learning culture and process-based knowledge management. In a learning culture, education is a ubiquitous thread, woven into every task; and it is both encouraged and rewarded. A company with a learning culture is constantly preparing itself to adapt to changing business conditions, and this is possible because its employees never stop learning, growing, and innovating, enabling it to respond instantly to new customer needs.

Just as important is the development of process-based knowledge management. In Zero Time companies, workers and processes are closely linked, and knowledge is *delivered* to workers at the time of need. In other words, the knowledge is parsed into small, easily understood *nuggets,* which the worker can instantly learn and use. Because there is no delay involved with this type of learning, companies that have mastered the Instant Learning discipline are able to outperform their competitors, which struggle with unwieldy training programs and knowledge databases. Figure 1.4 summarizes the essence of the Instant Learning discipline.

Knowledge is parsed into small, easily understood *nuggets,* which the worker can instantly learn and use.

Instant Adaptation

In today's constantly changing e-business environment, enterprises committed to traditional business practices find themselves engaged in a never-ending game of catchup. Most are unable to organize their workforce to be both disciplined and flexible. Managers in these companies face the common challenge of offering employees the freedom of empowerment while ensuring that they all strive for the same goal. For example, in the past, Hewlett-Packard had 40 divisions that

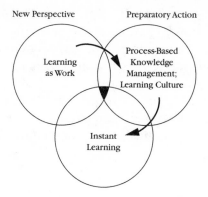

Figure 1.4 Essence of the Instant Learning discipline.

produced competing products, an example of the company's then widespread but uncoordinated empowerment policy. Likewise, GM's multiple overlapping products from various divisions diluted the company's original innovative strategy of one car for each income stratum. The current approach of people empowerment is insufficient since the actions of empowered people are often at cross-purposes with each other. Empowerment alone often causes competition, rather than cooperation, within the organization. At the same time, companies struggle to give employees the information they need to make informed decisions, while increasing their responsibilities as the new demands emerge at an always faster rate. Clearly, empowerment is not enough.

Zero Time companies practice the discipline of *Instant Adaptation*, which, while fully empowering individuals to create value for the customer, also aligns them with the group purpose and direction. To achieve Instant Adaptation, companies need *holonic* management. In holonic management, each part of the organization, from individual workers to teams to entire departments, is a complete entity operating within the whole of the organization. Each of these entities (or *holons*) within the whole, operates independently; it is given complete knowledge, control, and responsibility to produce value for the customer. Each holon, guided by knowledge and granted full responsibility, takes the most appropriate action in response to changes in the business environment. These holons are comparable to structures in nature, where each individual cell, a whole within the whole, possesses the genetic code for the entire organism. The Instant Adaptation discipline encourages companies to see and organize their businesses holonically for maximum flexibility and adaptation.

To achieve instant adaptation, companies
need holonic management.

To keep the holons within an organization in alignment rather than in competition with each other, the Instant Adaptation discipline teaches organizations to develop the core competencies of constancy of purpose and a trusting culture. Constancy of purpose keeps every holon focused on the overall good of the organization, which prevents individual holons from interfering with each other; a trusting culture enables the organization to adapt quickly, without micro-monitoring from management. Companies that have mastered Instant Adaptation are able to mobilize their workforce like a school of fish, with each holon taking appropriate independent action, while, as a group they move in the same direction. Figure 1.5 summarizes the essence of Instant Adaptation.

Instant Execution

Zero Time companies need processes that can be executed instantly. Therefore, Zero Time managers design processes that are free from resistance from all sources. Human intervention

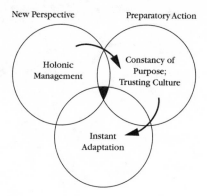

Figure 1.5 Essence of the Instant Adaptation discipline.

and boundaries tend to create resistance and delay, so Zero Time companies institute "no touch, no boundaries" processes that operate without human intervention and across boundaries. Designing processes in this way improves on the approach of simply automating processes. The application of technology alone rarely is enough to create processes that can be executed instantly. With the "no touch, no boundaries" standard, processes flow without resistance throughout the company as easily as electrical impulses flow through superconductors. We call this discipline *Instant Execution.*

Zero Time companies create "no touch, no boundaries" processes that operate without human intervention, and across boundaries.

To build "no touch, no boundaries" processes, companies must include both agility and the zero defects standard. Agility enables companies to reconfigure current processes or create new processes instantly in response to changes. The

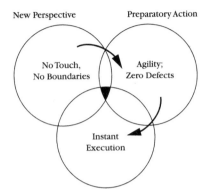

Figure 1.6 Essence of the Instant Execution discipline.

zero defects standard ensures that process outputs meet the customer's exact specification—every time, all the time. Figure 1.6 summarizes the essence of Instant Execution.

Instant Involvement

Having been debilitated by low-quality parts, delivery delays, and conflicting goals, the symptoms of a disconnected supply chain, companies today realize that to trade inventory information they must automate their supply chains. However, automation alone is rarely enough, since today's supply chain management approach fails to encourage the mutual commitment and shared risk that are the hallmarks of true successful partnerships. Zero Time companies make extensive use of the global e-business infrastructure to connect to suppliers; they also take extra steps to ensure success by developing meaningful partnerships. We call this discipline *Instant Involvement*.

Rather than viewing suppliers as separate entities connected by computer networks, Zero Time companies see themselves, suppliers, complementors (companies that produce complementary products), and customers as parts of the same ecosystem. If any member of the ecosystem fails, the entire ecosystem

---

Zero Time companies see themselves, suppliers,
complementors, and customers as parts of
a single ecosystem.

---

suffers. In such a tightly connected environment, all necessary parties are automatically involved, regardless of whether they are customers, complementors, or suppliers.

Unity of thought and action, without additional bureaucracy, is achieved through trusting strategic partnerships and mutual commitment. To strengthen the ecosystem, companies practicing Instant Involvement choose their strategic partners wisely, based on complementary technologies and similar cultures, then funnel the majority of their business to these partners. In addition, these companies share vast amounts of information on new products, industry trends, and markets with their partners. A sense of mutual commitment, including shared risk and deep trust, grows from these partnerships; this results in blurred boundaries, so that it becomes difficult to separate the company from its suppliers and complementors.

Intel Corporation and Cisco are famous for creating such tightly woven ecosystems. Such elite companies are equally dedicated to partnerships with their customers. For instance, Toyota, Boeing, and Intel are known to invite their customers to take an active role in the design of their next-generation products. Such closely connected companies are clearly better prepared, and thus faster to act, than their counterparts, which are still trying to repair their broken supply chains.

Companies that see the ecosystem as the only model for mutual success, and that take the time to develop strategic relationships based on mutual commitment achieve Instant Involvement. They move and change as a single unit in response to the business environment, in Zero Time. Figure 1.7 summarizes the essence of Instant Involvement.

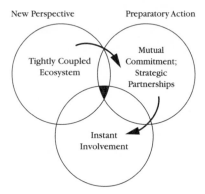

Figure 1.7 Essence of the Instant Involvement discipline.

Tomorrow's Winners

In December 1999, the magazine *Fast Company* reported the results of a poll in which readers were asked, "Does your company work in 'Zero Time?'"[3] Over one-third of respondents, 38 percent, said yes. That number will continue to increase as more companies recognize the need to operate in Zero Time. Undoubtedly, the Internet is the vehicle that will launch many previously elite but not yet Zero Time companies into the stratosphere of lasting success. And it will be the middle managers and executives who pursue in earnest the five Zero Time disciplines that determine whether an organization will be truly a Zero Time company.

The willingness of Zero Time leaders to act on what they see is priceless.

The managers who are beginning to build complete Zero Time organizations will become the leaders of the next wave of business change. They will guide the next generation of pioneer companies—the next amazon.com, Dell Computer and eToys—to market dominance. Zero Time managers will take unusual, innovative, even outrageous actions because they will see differently, then act instantly. They are preparing for a future that few others yet see. These managers understand that the only certain fact about their business environment is that it will change. Today's environment is already different from yesterday's, and tomorrow's will differ from today's. They know that to prepare for tomorrow they must be prepared to act instantly. They must master the five Zero Time disciplines to position their companies for the future. Managers who understand Zero Time thinking will be the leaders of tomorrow's winning companies, because time is on their side.

CHAPTER

The Quest

SONY'S INTRODUCTION OF THE WALKMAN NOT ONLY SHATTERED the perception that Japanese products were cheap and inferior, it catapulted the company into the position of a technological pacesetter. More important, within a few short years of its introduction, the Walkman triggered a revolution in the music industry: Cassettes replaced LPs and 45s as America's most popular media for recorded music. Twenty years and 250 million units later, the Walkman remains a dominant product line with more than 600 products under its banner.

But perhaps the most remarkable fact in the history of this immensely successful product is that, at its inception, Sony's co-founder, Akio Morita, had difficulty convincing his project team to even support its development. At that time, no one perceived that, in the future, customers would embrace a technology that enabled them to listen to music anywhere, any time, in private.[1] Moreover, according to Kozo Ohsone, general manager of the Tape Recorder Division, and in charge of the Walkman project, the general perception at that time in Japan was, "Anything you put in your ears to hear with, including headphones, was associated with impaired hearing, and deafness was a taboo subject."[2]

Morita, like all visionary leaders of elite companies, saw a "white space" of unarticulated consumer needs; in this case, a market composed of people who listened to music through headphones to create space and solitude in the midst of their frenetic lives. Diverging from the music industry's direct progression toward the proliferation of LPs and 45s in an established marketplace, Morita saw the future at a different angle, which enabled him to pioneer a completely new—and empty—marketplace in which Sony could be first, could dominate. The Walkman was launched in Japan in July 1979, and promoted as introducing a new "headphone culture."[3]

Being first allowed Sony to accumulate lead time, to establish technology, name, and product recognition before other competitors arrived in the marketplace. Hence, Sony established a solid customer base for its 80-plus models of increasingly portable stereo players, launched between 1979 and 1990. So dominant was Sony that, to competitors entering the cassette tape arena, it appeared able to offer new products and services instantly. This is the value of gaining time to prepare for the emerging market.

Morita saw a future in which people listened
to music through headphones to create space and
solitude in the midst of frenetic lives.

To further solidify its dominance in the cassette music market, Sony introduced a family of related and compatible products. Capitalizing on its core competency of miniaturization coupled with continuous innovation, Sony produced ever smaller and better products. The product-family strategy enticed customers who, for example, bought a Sony cassette product to buy others; they were attracted by the name recognition of the Sony product line. Later arrivals to the marketplaces, such as Toshiba, were locked out of the majority of the customer base—and, thus, profits.

The Walkman story illustrates the essence of a
Zero Time company: See a new white space
and act on it instantly!

Sony characterizes a Zero Time company. Its strategy for perpetual market lock-in perfectly demonstrates many Zero Time concepts. Merely seeing a future divergent market is not enough. Morita did not only perceive that a white space existed for the Walkman; he also moved quickly to prepare for anticipated competition. Having temporarily locked in customers and locked out the competition with its lead time, Sony solidified its market leadership with on going product innovations, making it less likely that consumers would switch their loyalty to another company. The Walkman story captures the essence of a Zero Time company: see a new white space and act on it instantly! Figure 2.1 depicts this essence. The solid arrow in the figure represents the predictable path of traditional market leaders, who are focused on extending their current market space; the dotted arrow represents a Zero Time company veering off the beaten path to explore a new white space.

Intercepting the Future

The purpose of this chapter, then, is to describe conceptually the path to becoming a Zero Time company. Zero Time companies must continuously perceive and intercept new market white spaces, which often requires radical strategic decisions

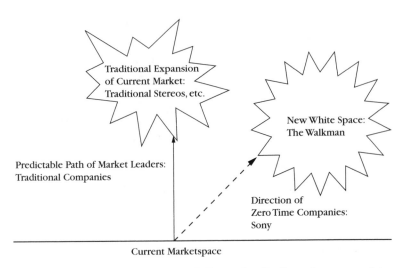

Figure 2.1 Essence of seeing differently: finding the new white space.

to tackle completely new markets. Intel, for instance, "... made the most crucial strategic decision of its corporate life in 1985, to focus the whole company on microprocessors and get out of the memory business it had invented."[4] NEC made a similar shift when Koji Kobayashi decided to forgo the company's primary business of producing nuclear reactors, and develop products for the computer and communications market, which was still in its formative stages. Both Intel and NEC are thriving today as a result of these abrupt changes.

Zero Time companies continually perceive
and intercept new "white spaces."

Other companies, following straighter, more traditional pathways of growth and expansion in existing markets, have not fared so well. Former powerhouses such as IBM, GM, Kodak, and

Xerox, blinded by their success, took the traditional approach of simply extending current product lines. They were unwilling to examine major strategic changes until their success began to wane. These companies were captives of the traditional S-curve of organizational growth that consist of four phases:

1. Infancy.
2. Growth.
3. Maturity.
4. Old age.

Other companies, following straighter, more
traditional pathways of growth and expansion
in existing markets, have not fared so well.

Zero Time companies, on the other hand, escape inevitable decay by turning their attention to often radically different or new markets before they ever reach the peak of success in existing markets. Essentially, Zero Time companies jump-start a new S-curve before they reach market leadership in current strategic areas. Figure 2.2 shows how Zero Time companies bridge the gap between current and emerging markets by accumulating lead time and investing in core competencies. As a result, Zero Time companies are able to create new markets, accumulate lead time, and dominate. We call this strategy the *interlocking S-curve.*

Zero Time companies escape inevitable decay by
turning their attention to new markets before they
ever reach the peak of success in existing markets.

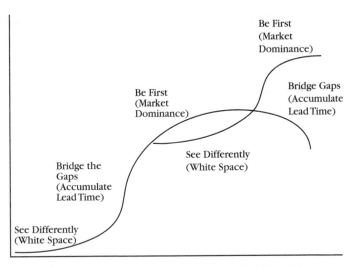

Figure 2.2 The interlocking S-curve for Zero Time.

In the late 1970s, another elite company, General Electric, awash in cash and facing no strong competitors, was nearing the pinnacle of maturity in its current markets. Rather than resting on its laurels, however, CEO Jack Welch kicked off a second S-curve in 1981 by directing the company to new white spaces. Welch introduced GE products and services to global markets, tore down internal boundaries, and ventured into new growth businesses such as technology, financial services, and news media. By voluntarily adopting the strategic changes necessary to intercept new markets in unoccupied white spaces, GE avoided the wrenching, painful upheavals experienced by the likes of IBM and GM.

Zero Time companies purposefully seek to break away from industry trends, which tend to form a direct and predictable path from present to future; they choose to intercept the future at a new angle, at the junction of white space. To succeed in this effort, Zero Time companies employ the following interlocking S-curve strategy:

- *Find the white space.* Broaden horizons to approach the future from a new angle, and include nonrelated industries and markets. For instance, Xerox found its future in document processing, rather than pursuing the traditional copier manufacturing market.

- *Accumulate lead time.* Move quickly to infiltrate new markets first, and invest in core competencies to achieve early dominance once there. Dell, for example, won customer loyalty in the custom-built computer arena by investing in "made to order" manufacturing technology.

- *Achieve market dominance.* Capitalize on core competencies, early market lock-in, and innovative product offerings to discourage customers from switching loyalty to another company. For instance, more than 90 percent of the software applications are written for the Wintel architecture, which effectively locks PC customers into Intel and Microsoft products.

The successful development of each of the S-curves requires use of the five Zero Time disciplines described in Chapter 1 to develop the necessary organizational capabilities. The Instant Involvement discipline, as one example, encourages companies to create long-term partnerships with suppliers, customers, and complementors, (companies that produce complementary products) to form tightly integrated

---

Zero Time companies bridge the gap between the current and emerging future markets by accumulating lead time and investing in core competencies.

---

yet varied ecosystem with a broad scope of vision and experience. Once they've established fully integrated supply chains, Zero Time companies can move quickly to establish new markets and accumulate lead time while their competitors are

still enmeshed in existing markets. Finally, the Instant Involvement discipline encourages collaboration with complementors to produce a broad line of interconnected products
that lock in customer loyalty. The five Zero Time disciplines,
when integrated, vastly increase a company's ability to utilize
the interlocking S-curve strategy for success.

The T-Strategy: An Implementation Approach

In the quest to become Zero Time, the most successful companies to date, including Sony, have used the T-Strategy as an
effective implementation plan to intercept future markets.
Simply stated, the T-Strategy allows companies to replicate
the cycle of finding white space, accumulating lead time, and
achieving market dominance in multiple markets by leveraging their core competencies across these markets. Figure 2.3
depicts the generic T-Strategy model.

Consider Sony's success with the Walkman. Sony built the
product based on the Morita's vision of a new white space,
the "headphone culture," then invested in its core competency of miniaturization to accumulate lead time. Once Sony

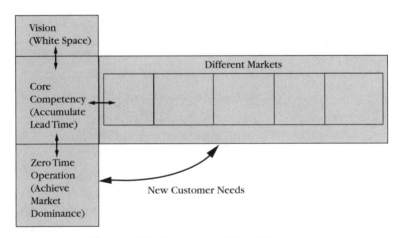

Figure 2.3 Structure of the T-Strategy.

The T-Strategy allows companies to replicate the cycle
of finding white space, accumulating lead time,
and achieving market dominance in multiple markets
by leveraging core competencies.

had achieved market presence with the Walkman, it quickly
leveraged its core competency to create other miniature products for numerous other markets in the music industry, from
cassette recorders to CD players. This rapid progress from
seeing the white space to leveraging core competency across
multiple markets is the T-Strategy in action.

Dell Computer Corporation, now leading the PC marketplace, offers another good example of this strategy. Dell's vision lies in its Direct Model, whereby the company sells directly
to customers and cuts out middlemen in the form of retailers,
resellers, and OEMs. Dell initially utilized this model in the
desktop computer market, then rapidly leveraged this model introducing a variety of products into the portable, server, and
storage device markets utilizing its core competency of the
build-to-order manufacturing process (see Figure 2.4).

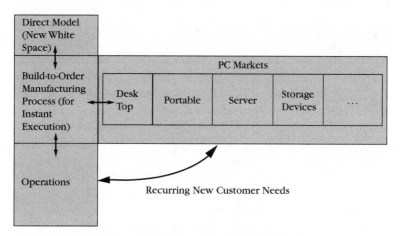

Figure 2.4 Dell Computer's T-Strategy.

Using the T-Strategy, a Zero Time company's core competencies are acquired during its precious lead time. Consequently, an organization can act instantly by introducing
multiple products based on the same core competencies into
many markets, sometimes concurrently. This strategy gives
companies a rapid, yet comprehensive, understanding of the
multiple markets based on the new white space. Such in-
depth understanding helps Zero Time companies recognize
which markets in the new white space are the best fit for its
core competencies, enabling the company to bring value to
customers in those market more quickly.

The Road Map to Zero Time Leadership

In the best-seller *Discipline of Market Leaders,* authors
Michael Treacy and Fred Wiersema describe three types of
market leaders: operational excellence, product leader, and
customer-intimate companies.[6] The value propositions and
core competencies of each type of market leader are described in Table 2.1.

Treacy and Wiersema argue that the cultures of each type
differ widely, making it difficult for organizations that excel

**Table 2.1   Value Propositions and Core Competencies of
Market Leaders**

Market Leader Type	Value Proposition to Customer	Core Competency
Operational excellence company	Guaranteed low price and/or hassle-free service	Excellent process execution
Product leader company	Leading-edge products or useful new applications of existing products or services	Innovation
Customer-intimate companies	Deliver specifically what the customer wants	Relationship cultivation

Source: Inspired by M. Treacy and F. Wiersema. 1995. *Discipline of Market Leaders.* Reading, MA: Addison-Wesley.

in one type of leadership to become another type. But we believe that these three types of companies are only steps along the way to becoming a Zero Time company. In fact, we think that each of the market leader types has mastered only two of the five Zero Time disciplines shown in Table 2.2.

Zero Time companies must go beyond
customer intimacy, operational excellence,
and product leadership.

Zero Time companies of the twenty-first century must go beyond market leadership, via customer intimacy, operational excellence, and product leadership. Figure 2.5 provides a road map of this evolutionary process. Each of these market leader types requires the deployment of two Zero Time disciplines, though not necessarily at full strength. For instance, customer-intimate companies clearly must have Instant Value Alignment with the customer. In addition, they must have Instant Involvement in order to coordinate with

Table 2.2   Required Zero Time Disciplines for Market Leaders

Market Leader Type	Core Competency	Zero Time Discipline Needed
Operational excellence	Excellent process execution	• Instant Execution • Instant Involvement
Product leader	Innovation	• Instant Learning • Instant Adaptation
Customer intimacy	Relationship cultivation	• Instant Value Alignment • Instant Involvement

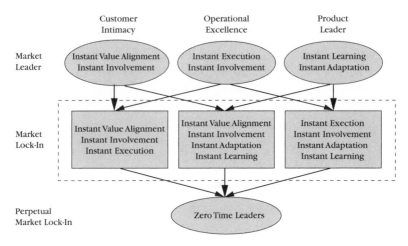

Figure 2.5 Road map to Zero Time leadership.

their suppliers and complementors for customer solutions. Operational excellence companies primarily need the discipline of Instant Execution, complemented by Instant Involvement for supply chain management, to achieve cost savings and prompt delivery. Finally, product leader companies need Instant Adaptation to empower individual creativity and innovation, along with Instant Learning to facilitate knowledge creation and use.

One step further than these three market leader types are the enterprises that deploy at least three Zero Time disciplines. We refer to these companies as having reached a position of *market lock-in,* meaning that they dominate the market, and have prevented competitors from achieving majority market share for the remaining life of the market. Intel, Sony, Microsoft, and USAA have achieved market lock-in in their respective industries. Amazon.com combined operational excellence with product leadership to achieve market lock-in in the online bookstore marketplace; Visa and Master-Card have combined product leadership and customer intimacy to lock out American Express, a long-time product leader that lacks the support of its partners in the retail business.

As companies move from market leadership to market lock-in to Zero Time, or perpetual market lock-in, the cost to customers to switch to another company continues to increase, as shown in Figure 2.6. And with the deployment of each additional discipline, companies are able to offer a broader, deeper, more customized product line, perhaps at a lower cost. For instance, companies with Instant Value Alignment have a thorough understanding of customer values, and provide highly customized products and services. Companies with Instant Involvement have a broad network of committed suppliers and complementors, which enables them to increase the breadth and variety of their product line. Companies with Instant Execution deliver their products and services rapidly and efficiently. The integration of all five disciplines gives Zero Time companies the ability to offer unparalleled products and services to their customers, and raises the switching cost for customers so high that loyalty is assured.

On the road to Zero Time, companies often undergo several transformations, as they shift from one strategic position

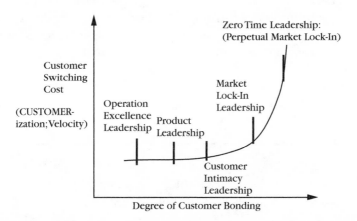

Figure 2.6 Customer bonding and switching cost at different stages.

to another. Geoffrey Moore, in his book *Inside the Tornado,* suggests that, in the high-tech industry, the evolution often begins with customer intimacy, whereby companies attempt to satisfy 100 percent of the needs of a particular group of customers.[7] In the next phase, high-tech companies broaden their focus to include multiple types of customers, and become product leaders. Once product leadership is ensured, companies become inundated with customer orders, and are forced to become operationally excellent to meet the demand.

While there is no predetermined path to Zero Time, the evolution primarily involves these stages:

- *Deploy more Zero Time disciplines.* The integration of each additional discipline brings the organization closer to Zero Time.

- *Deploy each discipline more fully.* As each new discipline is deployed, companies must extend current disciplines further. For example, in Instant Value Alignment, an initial deployment may be concerned with the direct customer, while an extension of the discipline would increase the scope to include the customer's customer.

- *Increase CUSTOMERization and velocity.* As multiple disciplines are introduced, the company rethinks its scope, to offer customized products and services, as well as to accelerate velocity to achieve Zero Time.

The evolution toward Zero Time involves the integration and harmonization of all five disciplines within the organization,

---

The integration of all five disciplines gives Zero Time companies the ability to offer unparalleled products and services to their customers.

---

with increasing levels of CUSTOMERization and speed. In the coming chapters, we will describe how elite companies are putting the Zero Time disciplines to work. More important, we will offer you guidelines to help you master each of these disciplines, one by one, in your own company.

The Holy Grail

The holy grail for a Zero Time company is more than customer intimacy, product leadership, or operational excellence. It is even more than market lock-in. For a Zero Time company, the holy grail is perpetual market lock-in, that is, perpetual market dominance in existing and yet-to-be-defined markets, brought about by instant CUSTOMERization.

When a company reaches Zero Time, it has the ability to see infinite market possibilities and intercept endless future markets.

When Sony's Akio Morita envisioned the white space for the Walkman, the company began to develop a dominant architecture that supported an entire family of products. Like Sony, amazon.com's Jeff Bezos envisioned a white space in which he would sell consumer goods through the Internet. Then he moved quickly to leverage his company's core competency—automated order fulfillment—across a number of markets. According to a *BusinessWeek* survey about online shopping, people think of amazon.com 80 percent of the time for books, 35 percent of the time for auctions, 21 percent of the time for electronics, and 37 percent of the time for music/video.[8] Amazon.com is approaching market lock-in (see Figure 2.7).

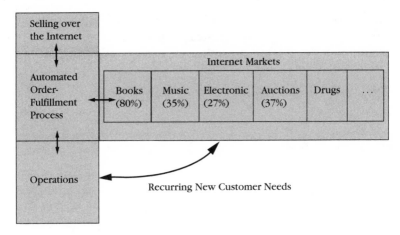

Figure 2.7 Amazon.com's T-Strategy.

Zero Time companies will consistently achieve market domination by interweaving new product and service releases with markets, via the T-Strategy. When a company reaches Zero Time, it has the ability to see infinite market possibilities and be the first to intercept these future markets. Zero Time companies are ever renewing, ever innovative.

3

Closing Value Gaps: Instant Value Alignment

THE CUSTOMER IS ALWAYS RIGHT. THE PROBLEM IS, MOST COM-
panies fall back on this adage when it's too late, when the
customer already has a complaint. Most companies lack the
vision to anticipate what will make an experience "right" for
the customer. Elite companies, those that will succeed in the
age of digital commerce, on the other hand, have a new perspective. They are constantly anticipating the future needs of
their target customers, then prepare to meet them *before* customers even know they need them. These companies practice
the discipline of Instant Value Alignment. The essence of this
discipline is described in Table 3.1.

Table 3.1   The Essence of the Instant Value Alignment Discipline

Current practice	Market share
New perspective	Customer share
Preparatory action	Deep understanding of customers
	Delight the customer

Current Practice Creates Value Gaps

Value gaps occur when there is a mismatch between what the company thinks the customer values and what the customer actually wants. This results in a never-ending cycle of catch-up, as the company, perpetually one step behind the customer, attempts to correct its mistakes by offering new products and services to meet the expressed needs, only to find that the customer is no longer interested.

Value gaps also occur when a company fails to adapt to changing customer needs because of its operational inefficiency. In today's digital world, processes and technology that support the "make to order" model for producing customized products and services are prerequisites to success. Companies without such infrastructure are in a perpetual downward spiral toward extinction, since today's customers demand—and are receiving—such customized, speedy service.

Companies often generate value gaps when they try to serve the mass market, and end up without a specific value proposition to their customers. No company can fully understand the needs and preferences of all its customers; elite companies know to carefully target a group of customers with similar values, a group they can profitably satisfy. For instance, SWATCH seeks customers who value fashion; Compaq delivers to those who expect quality; Home Depot provides outstanding service; and Harley-Davidson promises the trademark Harley-Davidson lifestyle.

Finally, value gaps occur when a company implements the traditional strategy of pursuing market share. In today's digital economy, the market is so fragmented that, in many

> In today's digital economy, the market is so
> fragmented that, in many industries, every single
> customer is its own market segment.

industries, every single consumer is his or her own market segment. The traditional approach of viewing the consumers in the mass market in terms of statistics is no longer viable. Indeed, by its nature, the value of market share is limited and temporary, since keeping market share requires ongoing expenditures, release of new and innovative products or services to continuously capture the short attention span of consumers, and massive marketing efforts to stave off competitors. Furthermore, the only way to increase market share is either to reduce prices or to increase spending on already expensive promotions. Neither of these options is guaranteed to generate permanent results.

The Instant Value Alignment discipline is about closing these gaps and realigning customer and corporate values. Instant Value Alignment companies know the customer is always right; more important, they know what is right for the

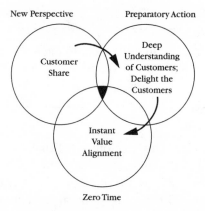

Figure 3.1 Essence of Instant Value Alignment.

customer. They align with customer values instantly by pursuing customer share, rather than market share, to achieve a deep understanding of their customers and delight them with unforgettable experiences during each transaction (see Figure 3.1).

Acting in Zero Time: Instant Value Alignment

At the heart of this discipline is the philosophy that the customer is always right. As such, Instant Value Alignment companies take great pains to understand their customers and develop customer share, which is defined as the lifetime business a customer is willing to give a particular company. These companies are able to instantly align with ever-changing customer needs, delivering what the customer needs almost before the customer has articulated the need to him- or herself. To accomplish such a feat, an Instant Value Alignment organization forms meaningful, long-term relationships with its customers, in effect bringing customers into the company's extended family. Like marathon runners in the race to win customers, Instant Value Alignment companies are long on stamina and patience, and are willing to take their time to attract valuable, lifetime customers.

Instant Value Alignment companies are long on
stamina and patience and are willing to take
their time in attracting valuable lifetime customers.

One indication of this customer intimacy is the frequency with which these companies collaborate with customers on crucial practices such as product development and business process redesign. These elite companies actively encourage their customers to provide feedback and guidance. Ultimately, this ongoing interaction with customers ensures a receptive marketplace for the Instant Value Alignment company's new products and services. Customers of Instant Value Alignment companies are brought into the corporate family, and their relationships with these companies are characterized by the free flow of information, custom-fit business processes, and frequent collaboration.

New Perspective: Win Customer Share

Instant Value Alignment companies go against the grain, putting very little effort into capturing market share. They understand that this concept views customers in each market segment as an undifferentiated mass, of which there is a limited supply. Hence, competitors battle against each other to win the maximum share of this limited commodity.

In contrast, Instant Value Alignment companies recognize that the number of customers may be limited, but that the amount of revenue to be earned from each customer over a lifetime could be substantial. These companies also understand the impossibility of satisfying the masses, which is the goal of market share. Instead, they expend their efforts to fully satisfy a smaller group of elite customers, who are willing to pay for highly customized services. From this perspective, Instant Value Alignment companies seek to win customer share, the lifetime business value of a single customer, from the right group of customers rather than market share.

Briefly stated, customer share is the volume of business a customer does with a certain company versus its competitors over the course of the customer's life. Companies treasure long-term customers, knowing it is far more profitable to sell additional products or services to the same customer than to sell the first product or service to a new customer. As such, Instant Value Alignment companies offer "unbeatable" service, to lock in customers for life; these companies make the cost of switching loyalties prohibitive.

For example, the Hertz Corporation locks in customer loyalty by offering unsurpassed service and convenience to its "time-compressed" business travelers in the Hertz #1 Gold Program.[1] Gold members step off the plane, bypass rental counters and long lines, and are escorted to their car, which has lights on and engine started. Self-serve map kiosks print out multilingual detailed directions to any destination. Hertz also outfits a special group of cars with the trademark "NeverLost" Global Positioning System, to appeal to consumers responsive to electronic gadgets. Returning a car can take under two minutes as waiting agents process mileage, gas level, date of return, and payment on a handheld computer—often under a roof that protects customers from the weather. With the Gold Program, Hertz wins customer share, because once customers become spoiled by the hassle-free experience of this program, they are unlikely to go elsewhere.

While the number of customers may be limited,
the amount of revenue to be earned from each
customer over a lifetime is far from limited.

Clearly, the return on investment for pursuing customer share is significant. The downside is that pursuing customer share requires patience and considerable expenditure. Instant Value Alignment companies use three basic tactics to guarantee success in this arena: select the best customers, establish long-term relationships, and create value for their customer's customer (see Figure 3.2).

Select the Best Customers

Instant Value Alignment companies are always on the lookout for time-sensitive customers, who value immediacy and elite service. These are the best customers, willing to pay

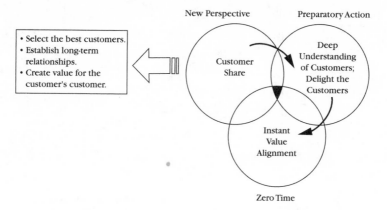

New Perspective | Preparatory Action

• Select the best customers.
• Establish long-term relationships.
• Create value for the customer's customer.

Customer Share

Deep Understanding of Customers; Delight the Customers

Instant Value Alignment

Zero Time

Figure 3.2 Instant Value Alignment: new perspective.

high dollars for outstanding treatment. These customers have become so accustomed to having their specific needs met—and exceeded—that they rarely even consider the competition for the same products or services.

Consider the case of Custom Research, Inc. (CRI), a Minneapolis-based research company.[2] In 1988, for the first time after 14 years of continuous growth and expansion, it experienced no growth. Puzzled and concerned, top executives at CRI studied their customer base to ferret out reasons for the company's sudden and unexpected stalemate. They were shocked to discover that CRI had *too many* customers, most of them were not profitable to service. CRI did not have the right kind of customers, those who are high-value and high-margin, to support the continued growth of the company.

In fact, of CRI's 157 total customers, only 10 met the high-value, high-margin criteria. CRI's target customers, who consistently purchased CRI's services at the highest margins, made up less than 7 percent of CRI's total customer base. Weighing in at the other end of the scale, 101 customers fell into the low-volume, low-margin category, swallowing up company resources by buying only low-margin services at infrequent intervals (see Figure 3.3).

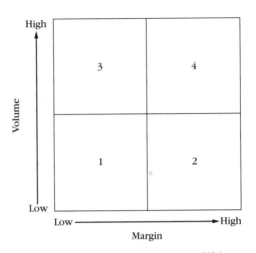

Figure 3.3 CRI's quadrant analysis.

At the end of the day, CRI was spending the majority of its resources servicing the low-volume, low-margin customers (first quadrant), who not only failed to generate a profit, but who actually cost the company to service. This then meant the company lacked the resources to appropriately service the high demands of their best customers, who ultimately generated the majority of CRI's profit. Subsequently, then, these best customers, known generally as fourth-quadrant customers, became CRI's target market.

In response to this revealing analysis of their customer base, CRI executives leapt into action, quickly disengaging from low-profit clients and focusing attention on their best customers. CRI executives created a group of services tailored to meet the specific requirements of these customers, designed to increase repeat sales from them. The company even organized elite "surprise and delight" teams to pamper and interact one on one with each valued customer. The result? CRI has doubled sales and profits from its 1987 levels and now boasts an impressive client list. Now, 36 of its best customers account for 86 percent of total sales and 96 percent of all profits. By taking pains to identify and understand its top customers, CRI reaped the benefits of high profits and reduced effort. CRI is an excellent example of the advantages of reducing the burden of servicing customers by catering to just one category of client—the "best."

Elite companies carefully select a group
of customers with similar values whom
they can profitably satisfy.

Like CRI, Instant Value Alignment companies are careful to pursue customer share with only a select set of customers. Because winning customer share can be a labor- and resource-intensive proposition, they usually target the fourth-quadrant customers, who are willing and able to offer the company significant revenue streams in exchange for fully customized service.

Establish Long-Term Relationships

In today's business climate, where business deals are no longer sealed with a handshake, but are accompanied by lawyers and piles of contract documents, Instant Value Alignment companies patiently cultivate and nurture their relationships with the elite clients they want to keep for life. Long-term customer relationships are the foundation for instant customer alignment, since instant alignment implies a high level of familiarity and trust between company and customer.

Singapore's Economic Development Board (EDB), is an ideal example of an enterprise that can instantly align with client needs thanks to its long-standing client relationships. The EDB is charged with the task of sustaining and increasing Singapore's economic growth, which is no easy task, as Singapore faces increasing pressure from the low-cost manufacturing sites that are sprouting up in neighboring countries such as Indonesia, Thailand, and China. EDB clients, companies that originally moved their manufacturing facilities to Singapore to take advantage of the lower manufacturing costs, expressed growing concern about the increasing cost of manufacturing in Singapore, meanwhile researching the possibility of moving their manufacturing facilities to neighboring lower-cost countries like Indonesia.[3]

The EDB's challenge lay in developing a strategy that would keep clients loyal, and sustain the revenue flowing to Singapore, while empowering its clients to take advantage of the low-cost manufacturing available in neighboring countries. Fortunately, the EDB has expended immense effort in developing a broad and deep network of long-term relationships with its clients. The EDB responded by cashing in on this well-tended, carefully monitored network of relationships, using this "grapevine" to start a series of collaborative dialogues with corporate clients. EDB clients, accustomed to such dialogues and information exchange through long association with the EDB, participated without hesitation, offering invaluable suggestions, input, and advice based on their own needs.

Ultimately, the collaboration produced the *regionalization* concept. Regionalization meant that Singapore would clone its highly efficient, well-managed industrial parks in lower-cost regions, which would lower the cost but maintain the quality at industrial facilities for EDB clients. Guided by this new concept, the EDB began building turnkey, utterly practical, and cost-effective industrial parks in the neighboring low-cost countries of Malaysia and Indonesia. EDB clients happily relocated their manufacturing operations to the new locations, while keeping their corporate headquarters, and their loyalty, within Singapore.

The EDB reaped huge rewards from its long-term, carefully nurtured relationships with corporate clients. Having direct access to clients who had developed deep loyalty to the EDB, and who willingly offered advice and active help, enabled the

EDB to align rapidly with customer needs by developing the regionalization concept. This collaboration, the result of well-established relationships, produced noteworthy beneficial results for all parties. The EDB is a good example of a Instant Value Alignment organization that has leveraged long-term relationships to align quickly and deliver customer gratification.

Create Value for the Customer's Customer

Instant Value Alignment companies are able to align themselves with the customer because they go beyond providing value for their customer, to create value for their customer's customer. Creating value for the customer's customer forces the company to become thoroughly knowledgeable about its customer, a prerequisite for instant customer alignment. Consider FedEx, which "absolutely guarantees" overnight package delivery. For the most part, it is not FedEx's direct customer, the sender of the package, who wants the package to arrive overnight, but FedEx's indirect customer, the receiver of the package, who desires such immediacy. Every time a package arrives on time, FedEx has created value for the receiver, the customer's customer, and aligned with the values of the sender, FedEx's direct customer.

Instant Value Alignment companies create
value for their customer's customer.

The partnership between Dell and UPS is another example of creating value for the customer's customer.[4] Dell focuses its attention on rapidly manufacturing customized computer systems, and relies on its partner, UPS, to deliver the computers with speed and accuracy. Dell and UPS have synchronized their systems tightly to ensure that complete systems are delivered to customer sites on time, with minimum fuss. To that end, UPS stores Dell monitors in local UPS warehouses; computer towers and accessory parts are trucked directly from the factory floor to the customer. Despite having product parts in two locations, which are shipped separately, UPS and Dell have achieved an unsurpassed success rate in coordinating the deliveries so that the computer, monitor, and accessories all reach the customers site at the same time. Dell reaps increasing customer share with each complete, on-time delivery, while UPS gains more business from Dell, resulting in a win-win partnership.

Intel achieves win-win partnerships of a different type with its customers, creating collaborations that initially seem counterintuitive and out of sync.[5] Intel collaborates with independent software vendors, despite the fact that the chip manufacturer neither buys nor sells products from these vendors. Why the collaboration? Intel recognized that PC consumers were purchasing an entire package consisting not just of Intel's microprocessor, but also of preinstalled software from Microsoft, Intuit, Adobe, and others. If any of the preinstalled software components fails to work well with the other software components, PC consumers may become dissatisfied, causing not only the software companies to lose sales, but Intel as well. So in spite of not having any direct connection with the vendors of preinstalled PC software, Intel works closely with these vendors to ensure that the products, when used together, deliver a positive experience to the customer. Intel looks beyond it direct customers, companies like Acer, Compaq, and Dell, to collaborate with companies that have an indirect impact on Intel's ability to win customer share.

Instant Value Alignment companies are not afraid to get involved with their customers on an intimate level because it brings them customer share. They are proactive when it comes to turning away business that will not result in lifetime customers. For those elite customers they do choose to serve, Instant Value Alignment companies offer fully tailored services not just for their direct customers, but for their customer's customer as well.

Preparatory Action: Understand and Delight the Customer

Instant Value Alignment companies excel because they see clearly the next wave of customer trends, which affords them the time to invest in core competencies. Developing these core competencies subsequently enables them to align instantly with customer values, to offer products and services that match these values. Instant Value Alignment companies focus on developing those competencies that support their mission of understanding and delighting the customer; these include dialoguing and collaborating with customers, to ensure a memorable experience, and building customer communities of value (see Figure 3.4).

Achieve Deep Understanding of Customers

Unlike companies that launch massive surveys, marketing promotions, or ad campaigns in an effort to understand a broad range of customers, Instant Value Alignment companies sift through their customer database and target only the customers

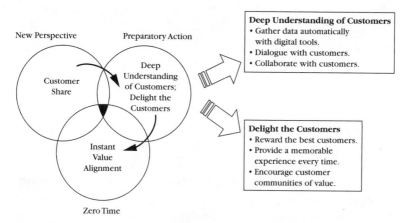

Figure 3.4 Instant Value Alignment: preparatory action.

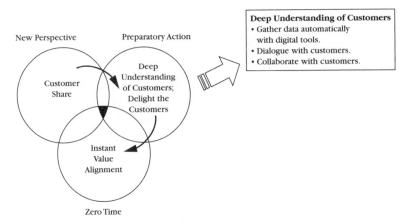

Figure 3.5 Preparatory action: deep understanding of customers.

they *want* to understand. These customers are the cream of the crop, customers who have the highest requirements and who purchase products and services with the highest margin. Instant Value Alignment companies relentlessly work to understand their best customers on three levels. Most superficially, Instant Value Alignment companies leverage digital tools to constantly, though passively, gather information about their customers. On the next level, they engage in ongoing dialogue with customers. Finally, at the third level, they and their customers collaborate (see Figure 3.5).

Gather Data Automatically with Digital Tools

Instant Value Alignment companies want to understand their customers on every level. At the most passive level, Instant Value Alignment companies arm themselves with an arsenal of information technology, and automatically capture customer data at every interaction. Less intrusive and more subtle than direct dialogue with customers, data collection via digital tools can generate detailed customer profiles even from the briefest of interactions.

Dell's online information system, for instance, tracks, organizes, and stores the minutiae of customer preferences and needs gathered from the point of sale. Dell's customer profile includes each customer's price-sensitivity level; detailed delivery criteria (critical for most large customers); and preferences about preloaded software, hardware integration, and a host of additional services.[6] Dell's online information collection is so effective that a customer never has to specify the same information twice, but simply updates any information that has changed. Dell's clever use of digital tools reflects its deep understanding of its customer need for convenience.

Dell is not alone in this type of effort. McKesson, an independent pharmaceutical supplier, and Wal-Mart have also fully integrated digital data collection tools with their point-of-sale systems, as has the virtual bookstore amazon.com. Amazon.com accumulates data on the types of books each customer has purchased in the past, as well as books the customer has considered but did not purchase. The company then offers to send each customer e-mail notices when books similar to the ones considered or purchased by that customer are published. Amazon.com even offers this service to potential customers who have yet to buy a book from the company. Amazon.com takes digital data collection to its highest level, using the results to drive a marketing plan that addresses each customer as a marketplace of one.

Instant Value Alignment companies arm
themselves with an arsenal of information
technology and automation to capture customer
data at every interaction.

Instant Value Alignment companies are equally skilled at talking with their customers to obtain even more information. Instant Value Alignment companies dialogue with customers in an effort to see with the customer's eyes and from the customer's point of view.

Dialogue with Customers

Instant Value Alignment companies engage their customers in dialogue at first contact, not only to develop a thorough understanding of the customer's needs, but often as a preliminary test of whether the customer is a fourth-quadrant, high-value customer. They have found that clear and open communication through ongoing customer dialogue is crucial if they are to keep up with changing customer needs or to identify new classes of customers who may eventually become the next "best" customer. Cisco is one company who uses dialogue to actually create products and expand existing product suites.

Recall the CRI example. CRI is dedicated to working only with the most ideal clients, fourth-quadrant clients. It expends extraordinary effort to separate the high-value clients from the masses. Dialoguing with current and potential customers is one of CRI's most effective tools. In fact, the company never considers taking on a new client until an intense exchange of information has taken place, which often results in CRI recommending potential customers to another company. CRI "gatekeepers" take potential clients through a rigorous dialogue session, asking six revealing screening questions to determine whether the potential client will bring high value and high margin. CRI's six questions, along with their intent, are listed here.[7]

- How did you hear about us? Reveals whether the prospect is serious or just gathering information.
- What kind of work is it? Provides clues to the industry and scope of potential project.
- What's your budget? Determines the potential client's level of intent and commitment.

- What are your decision criteria? Exposes the prospect's decision-making authority.

- Who are our competitors? Maps out the competitive situation.

- Why are you thinking of switching to CRI? Uncovers the prospect's values and needs.

Based on this not-so-subtle data collection session, CRI gatekeepers sort the high-margin prospects from the prospects who do not fit CRI's criteria of an ideal client, which includes prospects who are just gathering information or who lack authority to make decisions. CRI gatekeepers helpfully refer any nonideal clients to indirect competitors, much to the surprise of both the prospect and the competitor. Prospects who do fit CRI's criteria are assigned a special team of consultants, who work with the new client on a permanent basis and who encourage continuous dialogue and information exchange between CRI and client in order to align with the customer's values. CRI maximizes the benefits of customer dialogue, using it to bring elite potential clients to the top of the stack and to scout for new requirements and needs from existing clients.

Another company, National Semiconductor, hit the jackpot when it began collaborating with its customers in this way, and realized that it was the design engineers, rather than purchasing agents, who were the controlling force behind purchasing decisions made by client companies.[8] The company learned that although design engineers have no direct purchasing authority, they do create all the specifications for new products, and in the process of designing new products, they specify parts by consulting a variety of parts catalogs and data sheets from various companies, including the catalog and data sheets from National Semiconductor. Once the engineers complete the specification, the completed form sails through the purchasing process without further input. Purchasing agents do not make changes to the specification, and thus have little or no influence on the decision-making process.

A deep understanding of customers grows from dialogue with them.

In response to this new information, National Semiconductor switched the focus of its sales and marketing campaigns from purchasing agents to design engineers, thus exercising influence where it has the most impact. Had National Semiconductor not inquired into its clients' decision process, the company would still lack even a fundamental understanding of its customer, thereby diluting the effectiveness of its customer acquisition programs. Instant Value Alignment companies like National Semiconductor never fail to take advantage of the free, valuable, customer information to be gained from simple customer dialogue. These collaborations are perhaps the most valuable interactions with customers, giving Instant Value Alignment companies the opportunity to stand in the customer's shoes. The deepest understanding of customer values grows out of such contact with customers.

Collaborate with Customers

Instant Value Alignment companies engage customers in active collaboration beyond dialogue to gain a deep understanding of their values and needs. The Instant Value Alignment company realizes that customers are more than willing to participate in new product development, for example, because they know their input will result in improvements valuable to their business. In fact, it is common for elite companies to enlist customers as active participants in their design teams.

Consider Boeing's 777 design team on which key representatives from airline customers like Cathay Pacific, United, Air

Nippon, and Japan Airlines were included from inception. The basic design considerations for the airplane were thus shaped by the more than 1,000 suggestions made by customers. Boeing totally aligns with its customers by incorporating customer preferences and desires during the design process.

Nissan Canada collaborates with customers on another front, offering incentives to those who bring referral customers to purchase Nissan cars and trucks.[9] In 1990, Nissan Canada found it had a very low customer retention rate. The company reacted by designing a generalized customer satisfaction program, centered around friendly and responsive service, which it promoted on a massive scale. Because the program was so general, and attempted to appeal to a broad range of customers, the results were disappointing. Nissan Canada realized it had to be more specific in targeting customers, that it had to research the needs and preferences of each specific customer group.

As a result of more in-depth research, the company developed a new approach that focused on the establishment of long-term, collaborative relationships with *existing* customers who were satisfied with Nissan products. Customer service representatives and salespeople were instructed to form lasting, personal relationships with their customers. This approach was much more successful. Not only did Nissan Canada retain more customers, it also garnered a roster of satisfied customers who were then motivated to refer new customers. Nissan Canada is leveraging this trend by launching additional marketing campaigns that offer satisfied customers incentives to send even more referrals. In the case of Nissan Canada, trial and error eventually resulted in a collaborative strategy, one that involved existing customers, which helped the company align with the customers who want a personal relationship with their Nissan representative.

Instant Value Alignment companies know to examine the entire scope of the customer experience, and then aim to exert the maximum influence over as many areas as possible.

Instant Value Alignment companies use collaboration not only to increase their awareness of customer values, but also to bring the customer into direct contact with the product development process. These companies have found collaboration to be one of the surest ways to produce products and services that match the current and future needs of their customers.

Delight the Customer

Having gained a thorough understanding of their customers through the preceding core competencies, Instant Value Alignment companies are quick to develop those skills that will enable them to provide memorable, satisfying experiences for their customers. These top companies have come to realize that creating a memorable experience at every customer interaction is one of the most effective strategies for increasing customer share. Instant Value Alignment companies focus on developing the core skills that allow them to reward their best customers, provide an unforgettable experience, and build customer communities of value (see Figure 3.6).

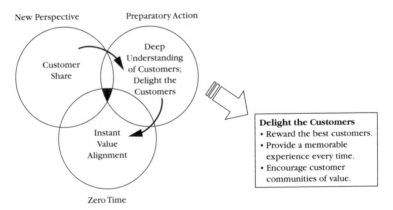

Figure 3.6 Preparatory action: delight the customer.

Reward the Best Customers

Instant Value Alignment companies know that one of the easiest ways to win customer share is to reward their best customers in the form of significant incentives. However, these companies offer the best incentives to only their top echelon of clients, and institute rather high requirements for earning these top incentives, so the number of rewards actually given is fairly low compared to the actual volume of business generated from this reward system. That is, these incentive systems encourage a major percentage of customers to aim for the reward, but only a small percentage actually earn the top rewards; the rest earn smaller, less costly (to the Instant Value Alignment company) rewards.

American Airlines is the perfect example of this strategy. It offers a wide range of rewards to its customers through the AAdvantage program. The AAdvantage program works on a sliding scale, meaning that the more often a customer flies, the more significant his or her reward. The most significant rewards are reserved for American's fourth-quadrant customers, the business travelers, who represent the top 2 to 3 percent of all airline travelers in volume and margin. American Airlines pursues customer share from business travelers with the utmost diligence.

For the business traveler, the airline offers three classes of AAdvantage cards: Gold, Platinum, and Executive Platinum, which require customers to earn 25,000, 50,000, and 100,000 points, respectively, each year (each point is worth about one mile flown). All Gold, Platinum, and Executive Platinum AAdvantage flyers may upgrade to the next class by paying a nominal fee or by using earned upgrade stickers. Executive Platinum flyers, the most frequent flyers, are eligible for the most meaningful advantages; they may request upgrades up to 100 hours in advance of the flight, giving them the best chance of getting the upgrade. Gold and Platinum flyers, respectively, must wait until 24 and 72 hours before their flight. American Airlines also guarantees that Executive Platinum members will always get a seat, as long as they book the flight at least 24 hours in advance; the airline also reserves some of the best seats on the plane for these top flyers.

The AAdvantage program is acknowledged as being the best in the airline industry, pulling in the largest share of high-value customers. American Airlines pays out only incremental cost to implement the program, and manages to lock in some of the biggest spenders, for life. For Instant Value Alignment companies like American Airlines, rewarding their best customers is their own reward.

Provide a Memorable Experience Every Time

Most enterprises know that customers value memorable experiences; fewer understand the ingredients of serving up such an experience. Instant Value Alignment companies find multiple ways to achieve this at every transaction, whether it's by offering Disney-like experiences, by allowing customers to control their own experiences, or by offering the stability of a brand-name experience.

For instance, in 1995, Dorothy Lane Markets, owner of two upscale supermarkets in Dayton, Ohio, wanted to increase the visibility of its stores by offering customers a Disney-like shopping experience.[10] However, Dorothy Lane employees were simply not trained to offer these types of experiences to customers in the course of their daily work; nor did Dorothy Lane have the training programs in place to support this effort.

In the end, CEO Norman Wayne was inspired to use theatrics to motivate his employees. Wayne turned "backstage jobs into center-stage performances," and Dorothy Lane employees into "local celebrities." He also encouraged each department to put on "shows" for shoppers to create a more memorable experience. As an example, managers in the wine and cheese departments now offer workshops, and stage wine shows.

Employees are also empowered with specialized training and given new roles with stagelike titles. From this dedicated effort, Dorothy Lane Markets has refocused its employees to deliver unforgettable encounters with customers, thereby encouraging repeat business and increasing Dorothy Lane's share of each customer's lifetime value.

Other Instant Value Alignment companies create a memorable experience for the customer by offering the stability of a brand-name experience. Many Instant Value Alignment companies, understanding that customers value standards and certainty, develop their brand names as a symbol of security, consistency, and ongoing quality. Singapore Airlines is well known for its brand-name commitment to service excellence.[11] Tan Chik Quee, an executive of operations at Singapore Airlines, explains the company's dedication to upholding its brand-name experience: "We constantly shave pennies from our cost structure in the back office. However, when we come to customer experience, we do not hesitate to invest because that is what Singapore Airlines is all about." Travelers ride with Singapore Airlines again and again because they know that the name Singapore Airlines stands for safe, comfortable, and convenient travel, combined with service excellence.

Only when customers win, by having their values met, in the time and place of their choosing, will you win the rewards of profit, growth, and leadership.

Because no company, not even an Instant Value Alignment company, can always anticipate customer needs, Instant Value Alignment companies often choose to allow customers to control their own experience. The *Wall Street Journal* offers its readers the ability to control the content of their online newspaper. Subscribers to the online edition can create a personalized version of the paper geared specifically to their topics of interest by specifying keywords and subjects of interest. The *Wall Street Journal,* in essence, becomes a clipping service for each subscriber, delivering a digital newspaper filled with only those stories that match the specifications set by the subscriber. In addition, through the online edition, subscribers are often privy to breaking stories from the Dow Jones News Service, stories that are not otherwise available.

In a much less dramatic but no less important way, Instant Value Alignment companies create a memorable experience simply by offering excellent services through well-designed, easy-to-use processes. Companies opting for this approach have discovered that their customers often value the convenience of a well-designed process more than the excitement of new or additional services. Instant Value Alignment companies are careful to examine the processes that affect the customer *from the customer's point of view,* to determine whether they meet customer needs. Processes that are poorly designed from the customer's point of view cause frustration and, hence, a poor opinion of the company.

For instance, when Dell began marketing and selling custom computers over the Internet, the company's biggest challenge was to design the Web pages from the customer's perspective. Michael Dell explains:

> *The hardest part was not the technology, but the behavior shift—for our own salespeople as well as the customers. Simplicity and convenience were paramount. We had to build an Internet system that was so convenient, customers got more value for their time than they did on the phone. That was the only way we could wean them off face-to-face or ear-to-ear contact. It was a high bar to clear.*[12]

Instant Value Alignment companies like Dell put their customer-directed processes through rigorous tests, garnering feedback from beta test groups, customer focus groups, and a variety of other customer input forums. The success of

Dell's online computer sales operation proves that the company has designed the online purchasing process to align with customer values.

Whether an experience is memorable to the customer because of its convenience, innovativeness, excellent service, or brand-name security, Instant Value Alignment companies never stop looking for ways to delight their customers. Because each Instant Value Alignment company develops ways to provide memorable customer experiences around its strengths, its core competencies, the result is predictable: satisfied customers and increased customer share.

Encourage Customer Communities of Value

Many Instant Value Alignment companies are exploiting the nation's addiction to online Internet chatting to delight customers by creating a virtual environment in which customers with shared values gather to exchange information, find companionship, be entertained, and learn. America Online (AOL) is perhaps the best example of such a company. AOL has opened cyberspace to the computer-illiterate, made it possible for nontechnical people to gather, learn, grow, connect, and hang out. AOL's easy-to-use technology has made it possible for a wide range of users to form communities of great value to them. Communities spring up around entertainment, education, cheap thrills, personal expression (one of the great liberties of being online anonymously) and timely information, all for a little more than $20 per month. These communities offer such significant value to users that AOL consistently captures a high percentage of customer share despite the availability of cheaper (even free) and more effective Internet and e-mail access. AOL also gets a voyeur's view of emerging trends, customer values, and the hot topics of the day by monitoring the content of chat rooms and bulletin boards.

Cisco Systems, which produces networking software, also has a community-based customer support Web site that enables customers to both provide input into CISCO products and to help other customers; the side benefit is that it also reduces Cisco's maintenance and customer support costs. In her book *Customer.com,* Patricia Seybold reports that Cisco's Web site processes between 350,000 and 400,000 transactions a month, while Cisco's call center volume remains flat, despite outrageous growth, indicating that the majority of Cisco customers are finding value in seeking answers to their questions online.[13] Cisco customers seem to prefer to get their answers from their fellow consumers, resorting to the call center only for complex problems that can't be handled through the online Open Forum. Cisco's continued growth and high rate of retention reflects the company's high customer share, a result in large part, of its creation of customer support communities online.

One way to entertain customers is to let them
control the customer experience.

Online communities, like Cisco's, build customer share for Instant Value Alignment companies by strengthening the consumer connection to them. Companies that pay attention to the workings of these online communities will find abundant opportunities for dialogue and collaboration with their customers. Therefore the benefits of online communities are: they automatically lower the cost of maintaining customers; and the constant customer feedback helps the company to incorporate these needs into future products.

Close the Value Gaps

In his book *The Age of Paradox,* Charles Handy describes his experience of a "Chinese contract." His counterpart, a Chinese gentleman, told him: "In my culture, a good agreement is self-enforcing because both parties go away smiling and are happy to see that each other is smiling. If one smiles and the other scowls, the agreement will not stick, lawyers or no lawyers."[14]

Underlying the Instant Value Alignment discipline is the basic principle of win-win. In order to be truly a dominant force in the market, you must gain the maximum customer share from all the customers you select by understanding and delighting them to the nth degree. Only when they win, by having their values met, in the time and place of their choosing, will you win the rewards of profit, growth, and leadership. To win in the marketspace, you will need to see from the customer's eyes by closing the value gaps to zero.

CHAPTER

FedEx: An Instant Value Alignment Company

FEDEX IS CURRENTLY THE LARGEST U.S. DOMESTIC OVERNIGHT delivery service, offering a series of package and air freight services, and delivering on time a stunning 99.5 percent of the time. The company employs more than 100,000 people, owns 35,000 trucks, and holds a staggering 50 percent of the U.S. market share for overnight delivery.[1]

The secret to the FedEx success is its People-Service-Profit philosophy. FedEx starts by hiring only the best people. Then the company seeks to maximize their motivation, performance, and value by offering state-of-the-art tools, wide-open career paths, and alluring incentives. FedEx works hard to create an entrepreneurial culture, with an employee stock purchase plan that encourages workers to own a stake in their business. FedEx employees, thus empowered, are authorized to develop relationships with customers and anticipate their needs, taking *whatever* steps are necessary to achieve 100 percent on-time delivery, 100 percent information accuracy and 100 percent instant customer gratification.

FedEx considers the clock to be its true competitor.

The company believes that from effective people and consistently high service quality, profit will follow. Above and beyond this philosophy, FedEx is an Instant Value Alignment company that understands its customers, is focused on winning customer share, and is able to sustain instant alignment with its customers' values. Laurie Tucker, senior vice president in charge of customer experience, summarizes the company's current value alignment: "The company has always listened to its customer. Now it's about anticipating the customer. There is no time for incremental improvements."[2]

Acting in Zero Time: FedEx Aligns Instantly with Customer Values

FedEx understands its customers' needs, and to meet them with products and services, which wins customer loyalty. The alignment with customer values occurs when FedEx flawlessly executes its processes to deliver packages around the world on time. In this way, FedEx provides what their customers value: reliability, speed, convenience, and personalized service.

The tightly disciplined, well-coordinated, and highly automated process enables near-instant alignment with customer values. Here's how it works: When a courier picks up a package from a customer site, he or she manually enters the destination zip code into the Supertracker, FedEx's handheld computer device, and scans the bar code off the package, also using the Supertracker, which records the package's unique tracking number. Upon returning to the truck, the courier downloads the information from the Supertracker to the FedEx global network; tracking begins within two minutes. Once the information has been downloaded, FedEx customer service personnel worldwide have access to all pertinent information about the package, including the time of pickup, the name of the courier, the location of pickup, the type of service, the destination, and the intended route. FedEx is able to align with the customer need to quickly track packages in a mere two minutes.

The package is then loaded from the truck onto an airplane, which flies directly to one of FedEx's regional HUBs, centralized locations where packages are sorted and reloaded onto planes that will take them to their final destinations. At each HUB, hundreds of planes arrive and depart between 11:00 P.M. and 2:45 A.M., carrying several hundred thousand packages to destinations worldwide. Thousands of FedEx employees work at each HUB, sorting packages on conveyor belts at a rate of 500 feet per minute. As packages are reloaded onto planes, each package is again scanned and the status of each package is again updated. The packages are also scanned when they arrive in the destination city and when they are placed in a van for final delivery.

The execution of the process results in alignment with the customer values of reliability, speed, convenience, and personalized service.

Upon arrival at the customer site, the package is scanned one final time for delivery confirmation, and the name of the receiver is keyed into the Supertracker. The package status is updated with final proof of delivery when the courier downloads the delivery confirmation information from the Supertracker to the global FedEx network.

FedEx ensures that the entire process, from scheduling a pickup to final delivery, is always in alignment with customer values. The FedEx process is geared to demonstrate speed, reliability, and convenience at every customer interaction, including interactions that do not involve personal contact. Today, FedEx is embracing the transforming power of the Internet to design compelling experiences for its customers. As Tucker sees it, "Our customers are moving at Internet speed, so they need us to respond at Internet speed."[3]

New Perspective: FedEx Wins Customer Share

In 1973, Frederick Smith saw a great opportunity for an efficient package delivery service that would transmit highly time-sensitive materials. Thousands of businesses valued the capability to move such packages anywhere in the world overnight. Smith capitalized on that opportunity by founding FedEx, a company aligned with the customer need for door-to-door, on-time, reliable overnight package delivery services.

FedEx sees its customers as those people
willing to pay reasonable dollars for on-time,
dependable delivery service.

FedEx considers the clock to be its true competitor. Its ability to retain customer loyalty stems from its obsession of using time as its primary defining measure. Smith views his business as that of delivering time-sensitive, high-priority items in the new economy, including life-saving medication, financial and legal documents with tight deadlines, or high-value materials. As such, FedEx sees its customers as those people willing to pay reasonable rates to guarantee on-time delivery of materials.

Having targeted this specific customer group, FedEx wins customer share by understanding time from the customer's point of view, with a goal of delivering in Zero Time. FedEx's relentless competition against the clock is demonstrated by its continuous improvement in delivery time:

1973: Delivers packages by noon the next business day.

1982: Delivers packages by 10:30 A.M. the next business morning.

1984: Offers a money-back guarantee for all packages arriving after 10:30 A.M.

1985: Offers a money-back guarantee for all customer packages not located within 30 minutes of inquiry.[4]

FedEx then realized that the ultimate time improvement would be gained by turning part of the process over to its customers. As a result, FedEx became the first company in the air freight industry to offer package-tracking information to customers. It was also the first company to post its package-tracking information on the Internet, and the first to offer an e-mail service that allows the sender of the package to notify the recipient that a package has been sent. In all of these ways, FedEx provides compelling experiences for its customers.

As more companies copy FedEx's innovations, FedEx continues to move into the next white space to provide more value for its customers. According to David Roussian, vice president of Electronic Commerce Marketing, FedEx is shifting away from the traditional transportation service, and into the supply chain market. He envisions that the market will shift from the movement of goods to the movement of information to the movement of flows and eventually to the management of flows. He adds, "At the end of the day, we need to treat transactions as flows and only manage flows."

Tom Schmitt, senior vice president of e-Supply Chain Services, articulates the evolving FedEx vision as "We want to be the supply chain of choice for our large customers. We want to be the number one partner in supply chain management." With this in mind, he believes that FedEx will become "a smart technology-enabled supply chain solution provider."

Preparatory Action: FedEx Understands and Satisfies Its Customers

FedEx has focused on developing the core competencies that enable it to understand and satisfy its customers all the time. FedEx demonstrates a deep understanding of its customers' needs, having studied the market closely and having culled a select group of customers who fit a specific fourth-quadrant profile (as discussed in Chapter 3), those customers willing to pay for elite, immediate, and dependable service. Brian Arnold, FedEx account executive, comments on his customers' needs: "Customer hot buttons are things like 'Can you save me time?' or 'Can you give me information?' or 'Can you help me help my customers?'" Top-tier FedEx customers demand speed of service, reliability, and constant access to information about the whereabouts of packages:

> *The person who ties the services all together in the field for our larger customers is the customer salesperson or consultant. He or she informs the large customer what services Federal Express provides that would be of interest to the customer.*[5]

Like most companies focused on Zero Value Gaps, FedEx uses information technology to serve more than one purpose. While its system certainly provides satisfaction to FedEx customers, the system also delivers detailed analyses on both general and company-specific shipping trends, which points the way to future customer needs and helps FedEx prepare for them. FedEx has built a mechanism for understanding customer values into its daily interactions with customers via its information system.

FedEx was the first company in its industry to offer an online tracking system to its customer, a service that aligns the company with its customers' need to track the progress of their package during the shipping process. FedEx provides its customers with turnkey systems such as FedEx Ship and FedEx Internet Ship, which facilitate shipping via the Internet. Today, more than 70 percent of the 3 million packages that daily move through FedEx's network are processed online.

In addition, FedEx is in the process of completing its One Call system, which enables cross-trained reps to solve complex customer problems without the assistance of specialists.

In its quest to satisfy customers, FedEx is dedicated
to continuously dialoging with the customer to
determine how products and services might
be improved to better serve the customer.

In addition to employing sophisticated technology to aid its customers, FedEx emphasizes the need to delight every customer by training its employees to recognize the importance of developing long-term customer loyalty. Cyndi Henson, Vice President of Customer Service, describes this attitude:

While the primary customer contacts are the customer service representatives and the couriers, everyone in the organization is a customer contact person. We are a customer service-dependent company, and everyone must pitch in to provide the best customer satisfaction possible.[6]

In its quest, FedEx is dedicated to continuously dialoguing with customers to determine how products and services might be improved to better serve them. FedEx customer consultants regularly call on high-volume customers to ensure they are satisfied with FedEx services, and to explore how the company might adapt and tailor those services to better meet the customers' specific requirements. For instance, FedEx has developed a relationship with L.L.Bean, the mail order clothing and outdoor equipment retailer. L.L.Bean, committed to delivering high-quality products on time to customers, chose FedEx to provide expedited package delivery service because of the FedEx willingness to customize its services to fit L.L.Bean's needs.

L.L.Bean spent so much time with logistics experts at FedEx and is so sure of FedEx's ability to deliver packages on time, that L.L.Bean began offering guaranteed delivery services. Being able to offer customers fast, reliable, and inexpensive delivery—as well as the ability to track the status of each shipment—greatly enhances L.L.Bean's customer share. The more customer share L.L.Bean wins because of FedEx services, the more customer share FedEx gains in return from L.L.Bean.

FedEx has formed another high-visibility partnership with Cisco Systems. In this new partnership, FedEx assumes full responsibility for the logistics of all out bound shipping for Cisco products. FedEx is also actively engaged in partnerships with the consulting firm KPMG as well as the technology firm SAP. FedEx is also partnering with other e-businesses to handle logistics tasks.

The more customer share L.L.Bean wins because of FedEx services, the more customer share FedEx gains in return from L.L.Bean.

To be a supply chain for their large customers, FedEx is completing an ambitious project of providing an integrated tool set on a common platform which can be easily tailored to the customer's needs. This complete and integrated tool platform is considered the key competitive advantage of FedEx in its evolution to be the supply chain of choice by its customers, according to Tom Schmitt.

FedEx is a complex, highly interconnected network system that requires discipline and focus to sustain. It takes approximately 17 hours for a package to travel from shipper to receiver. Within that 17 hours, FedEx must orchestrate an intricate dance, synchronizing customers, packages, couriers, trucks, planes, information, and a host of other moving parts. An array of locations, including the customer site, FedEx station, airport, HUB, and destination city must be tracked and organized for maximum efficiency. As a company with Instant Value Alignment characteristics, FedEx has pulled together these scattered resources, locations, and information to form a nimble, yet widespread organization in such alignment with customer values that customers turn to FedEx without a second thought when the package absolutely, positively has to be there overnight.

Messages for Managers

Companies like FedEx have taken extraordinary measures to practice the Instant Value Alignment discipline. We summarize the lessons they learned here.

- *Improve the ability to align with customer value.* Understanding the customer means understanding the customer's customer. FedEx has this perspective. It is delivering services that help make its customers look good to their customers. Customer-contact business processes are tuned for speed and convenience, using customer profiles to design tailor-made interfaces. At FedEx, workers are constantly challenged to think of new ways in which the company might interact with its customers digitally.

- *Use technology infrastructure to deliver value to customers.* The new features critical to Instant Value Alignment companies include at least the following:

  —Internet infrastructure, to facilitate e-commerce with customers.

  —Integrated customer database, to create a single, unified customer profile accessible to all employees.

  —Configuration rules engine, to allow customers to help themselves.

  FedEx continually upgrades its infrastructure. To keep pace with customer expectations, the company was the first in its industry to use the Internet.

- *Build a customer-centric culture.* FedEx consistently focuses on providing customer value. It gives customers control over their experiences by allowing them to interact directly with its online tracking system. And the culture is extended beyond the interfaces, since FedEx floods the organization with customer information. It encourages people to use it for everything from designing products and services to new interfaces for the customer.

Closing Learning Gaps: Instant Learning

TO SEE AND INTERCEPT THE NEXT "WHITE SPACE," AND TO DELIVER instant CUSTOMERization, Zero Time companies never stop learning. These companies have the ability to absorb every ounce of information from their customers and their environment, creating from that information the essential knowledge that becomes the next best-selling product or service. More important, these companies see learning as a part of work, rather than separate from work. For these companies, there is no gap between the acquisition of information and the translation of that information into products and services that produce customer value, and ultimately, market lock-in. Information is systematically acquired, sorted, labeled, filed, distributed, translated, used, and recycled so that nothing is lost.

Table 5.1   The Essence of the Instant Learning Discipline

Current practice	Learning is separate from work
New perspective	Learning as work
Preparatory action	Process-based knowledge management
	Learning culture

Therefore, whatever information is needed currently is instantly available. In short, Instant Leaning means using preparatory time to set up learning systems to enable Instant Learning.

> Companies that have mastered the art of
> Instant Learning never stop learning.

The best place for learning may not be a classroom at all. In Instant Learning companies, everyone is trained wherever they are, whenever they need it, and in whatever way is appropriate. At the Bank of Montreal, that means building a facility where individuals continuously learn in serendipitous meetings and informal conversations. At Andersen Consulting, that means using a CD-ROM-based best practices simulation for new consultants who want to learn by doing. At retailer The Limited, that means running game shows to train employees. The objective of this discipline is continuous, instantaneous learning by everyone in the organization. The essence of this discipline is described in Table 5.1.

Current Practice Creates Learning Gaps

Learning gaps occur when there is a disconnect between the information or knowledge the company has and the work done by the employees in the organization. We see three primary gaps. One is apparent from the perspective of the worker. A learning gap occurs when a worker lacks the information or skills to complete a work assignment and does not know where to look for the needed information. A second gap appears in knowledge management. Knowledge management systems are typically built to collect and store important company knowledge for use by the organization. But a gap occurs when that information stored in the knowledge management system is not easily accessible; for instance, when useful information in the knowledge management system is difficult to locate, or worse, is forgotten, when an opportunity arises for which that information could be of value.

The best place for learning may not
be a classroom at all.

Finally, a third gap occurs when learning activities are separated from knowledge management activities. In an ideal situation, the knowledge management activities collect and store information, while the learning activities disseminate information to the workforce. Learning gaps are created when information gathered by the company is kept in a knowledge management system, but not incorporated into training or learning activities. Learning ensures that the worker has the necessary skills and knowledge, and knowledge management is the process of managing knowledge, so these two activities must be linked in order to produce maximum value for both company and customer. In sum, learning gaps occur when the skill or knowledge required to complete a task is unavailable.

Traditional solutions for distributing knowledge to workers, such as classroom training or Just-in-Time (JIT) electronic training systems, do not solve these problems completely. Gaps appear when knowledge gained in a classroom setting is lost before it can be applied in the job setting. Gaps also occur when the worker must take time out of the workday for training, which distracts from productive work. Learning gaps appear when a class is not offered at the time the worker needs the knowledge or when the worker cannot find the necessary JIT training module to help him or her complete the task at hand.

Many organizations currently use JIT learning as a way of providing information to workers on demand. Under this model, when a worker needs knowledge or training to complete a process or task, he or she can immediately request and receive help. With Just-in-Time learning, the user *pulls* the knowledge as needed. However, though this strategy shortens the learning curve, it still causes learning gaps, since users must both know they need help and know where to obtain that help.

Consider the consulting firm (whose name is kept confidential) that spent millions of dollars developing a new knowledge management system, which provided the information for Just-in-Time learning, only to find that the system was too complex for most consultants to use. Consultants often spent days locating a piece of needed information. For example, one consultant was seeking examples from previous implementations of code that would fix an interface between two computer systems. She searched the knowledge management system, to no avail. She searched outside the knowledge management system, sent e-mail to others in the company, and asked colleagues in her immediate surroundings. No solution emerged.

Resolving to fix the system, she spent two weeks writing code for the needed patch. She then spent another week debugging it. When she finished, she made sure the database

---

There should be no gap between the acquisition of information and the translation of that information into products and services that produce customer value, and ultimately, market lock-in.

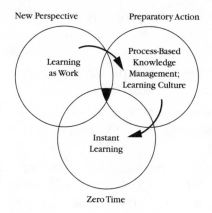

New Perspective   Preparatory Action

Learning as Work

Process-Based Knowledge Management; Learning Culture

Instant Learning

Zero Time

Figure 5.1 Essence of Instant Learning.

had the code in it for the next colleague. Two weeks later, an e-mail arrived from a colleague across the ocean, pointing her to code that would have fixed her problem. This example demonstrates one of the typical learning gaps that occur in companies that use traditional or Just-in-Time learning systems. Workers must know where the information is stored in order to access it in a timely manner.

The Instant Learning discipline bridges these gaps by encouraging businesses to see learning in a whole new light, and to develop core competencies that enable them to learn instantly (see Figure 5.1).

Acting in Zero Time: Instant Learning

At the core of a Zero Time company's ability to close learning gaps is its ability to instantly learn. Workers become immediately proficient at performing any required task; and if assistance is needed, it is instantly *pushed* out to the worker. We call this *Instant Learning*.

In Instant Learning, business processes and information systems are designed to track employee work, sensing when information might be useful, and pushing nuggets of knowledge out to the employee at appropriate times. The keys to success in Instant Learning are:

- *Information is automatically pushed to workers.* Workers do not need to search for help.
- *Information is pushed at the time of need.* Workers do not need to retain large amounts of materials learned in a formal class.
- *Information is parsed into easily digested knowledge nuggets.* Workers can immediately understand and use these nuggets, rather than have to learn and process large bodies of information at once.

For example, on the Toshiba assembly line for portable computers, the information system tracks each worker's progress in assembling computers. As the worker progresses, knowledge nuggets about quantity to build, along with instructions for each step are passively displayed on notebook computers placed at each assembly station. The worker reads these instructions and tips as needed, referring to them less frequently as he or she becomes more familiar with the assembly process.[1]

Because of the multiple benefits of Instant Learning, companies practicing this discipline reap a greater return on investment from Instant Learning than from traditional learning methods such as Just-in-Time or classroom learning. First, Instant Learning is embedded into the actual tasks performed by the worker, who does not perceive the situation as a training situation, but rather as job assistance. According to John Coné, vice president of learning at Dell Computer Corporation, workers view *job assistance* favorably, whereas they tend to resist *training.* So with Instant Learning, the learning event happens, but the worker does not perceive it as training.

Second, Instant Learning makes the appropriate information immediately available at the time of need. Unlike JIT training situations in which workers are forced to seek out the required information, or classroom learning situations where the worker must retain a larger body of information, instant training pinpoints the exact type of information needed and automatically delivers only that information.

Finally, an Instant Learning environment requires detailed study of business processes. This encourages companies not only to refine their processes, but to implement guidelines to ensure that processes are followed. Further, it encourages information, stored in the knowledge management system, be handled so it is useful to actual business processes.

Without a doubt, an Instant Learning environment can be expensive to implement. Examining and assessing business processes to highlight the areas where knowledge nuggets might be needed, continuously developing and updating knowledge nuggets, and creating systems to deliver the needed information all require vast expenditures of resources. But Instant Learning companies, having performed in-depth studies of the cost of training workers, realize that, long term, Instant Learning practices prove more cost-effective.

Terry Hill, regional training manager for Dell's national sales organization, illuminates the cost of offline training programs: "It can cost us $70,000 to $100,000 in lost sales if I pull people out of the field. Therefore, I spend a lot of my time working with them as a sort of coach while they are doing their job."[2] Similarly, with the high rate of turnover in many businesses, the cost of training new employees is high. But the cost of *not* training them is even higher. For Instant Learning companies, the cost of implementing an Instant Learning environment is a small price to pay to keep employees up to date, productive, and working.

New Perspective: Learning as Part of Work

Managers in Instant Learning companies approach learning differently, as a part of daily business practice, rather than as

> In Instant Learning companies, everyone is trained
> appropriately, instantly, and thoroughly wherever
> they are and whenever they need it.

a separate activity. Instant Learning occurs when needed information is pushed out to workers; workers learn automatically without having to stop to ask for help or to process the
information (see Figure 5.2).

Dell corporate documents describe Instant Learning with
the phrase, "Learning is synchronous with work."[3] Coné calls
this *stealth learning.* He explains in more detail:

> *The ideal "learning event" at Dell has a class size of 1,
> lasts 5 to 10 minutes, and takes place within 10 min-
> utes of when someone recognizes that he or she needs
> to know something. [That means it is delivered directly
> to that person at the moment it is needed.] Our chal-
> lenge is to reduce learning to its smallest, most-useful
> increments and to put the learner in charge of the en-
> tire process.*[4]

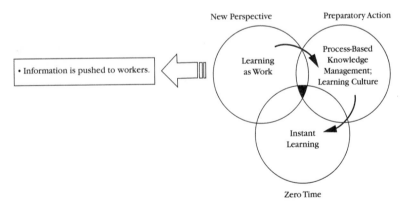

Figure 5.2 Instant Learning: new perspective.

Instant Learning companies have a vision of learning in which information is pushed to the worker. Business processes and information systems monitor the worker's progress, sense when information is needed, then automatically push the information to the worker. Instant Learning automatically delivers the right information at the right time, shrinking the learning curve to zero. In these companies, information is pushed rather than pulled, which redefines the process of learning.

Preparatory Action: Implement Process-Based Knowledge Management and Learning Culture

Recognizing the new way of learning is half the battle. Preparing for the implementation of this new way of learning requires investing in the core competencies that support Instant Learning. For Instant Learning companies, these competencies are

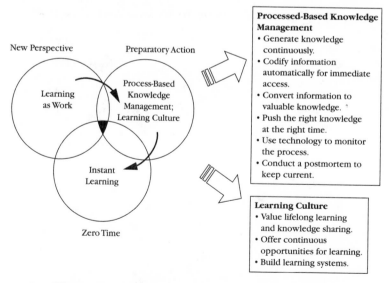

Figure 5.3 Instant Learning: preparatory action.

process-based knowledge management and a learning culture (see Figure 5.3).

Process-Based Knowledge Management

Instant Learning companies continuously strengthen their workers' ability to learn instantly by managing knowledge systems. Knowledge management is a three-step process that generates, codifies, and translates a vast quantity of information into the knowledge. But Instant Learning companies refine this process by managing knowledge in alignment with the processes in which that knowledge will be used. In other words, Instant Learning companies do not randomly gather pieces of information; instead they select only those nuggets of knowledge that will assist workers in completing tasks and interact with business processes more effectively. We call this *process-based knowledge management* (see Figure 5.4).

Instant Learning companies spend significant resources on process-based knowledge management, acknowledging that

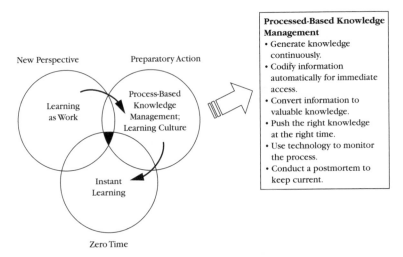

Figure 5.4 Preparatory action: process-based knowledge management.

the quality of products and services that result from Instant Learning are limited by the quality of information provided.

Knowledge management is a resource-intense endeavor, but Instant Learning companies mine such rich golden nuggets of knowledge to produce enormous cost savings and shorten time-to-market cycles; therefore, they consider the investment worthy. For instance, consulting companies including Ernst & Young, Andersen, and KPMG Peat Marwick have all reaped profitable rewards from managing the knowledge acquired from each consulting engagement and by codifying and distributing the knowledge through Lotus Notes and similar systems. By recycling corporate experience with knowledge management, the companies gain multiple returns on each completed project. Chevron has saved millions of dollars in annual fuel and power expenses by distributing internal knowledge on energy management. Pharmaceutical companies have developed a knowledge management system for getting products to market, recycling knowledge from past products, and substantially compressing the cycle time for FDA approval.[5]

Instant Learning companies painstakingly develop
their processes to automatically convert
information to value at the appropriate moment.

Knowledge management is the foundation for Instant Learning companies, providing the actual knowledge nuggets that produce instant customer gratification through excellent service and high-value products. They start the knowledge management process by generating information.

Generate Knowledge Continuously

Instant Learning companies are hungry for every scrap of information that potentially contains a valuable nugget to be translated into knowledge. In this first stage of knowledge management, they simply pull information from every available source, including interactions with customers, other companies or organizations, employees, vendors, and others. Further, electronic sources such as financial databases, industry databases, and other data repositories found on the Internet are valuable. The key is not to isolate information collection to either internal or exclusive interactions, but to pull information from any and all reliable sources.

Instant Learning companies are characteristically inventive and clever at generating information and at exploiting a wide range of sources. Tom Davenport and Larry Prusak, in their book *Working Knowledge,* describe five modes of generating information:[6]

1. Acquisition.
2. Dedicated resources.
3. Fusion.
4. Adaptation.
5. Knowledge networking.

Instant Learning companies regularly use all of these modes, plus two others:

1. Internal processes.
2. Customer interaction.

Table 5.2 summarizes and gives examples of each of these modes of information generation.

Instant Learning companies capitalize on both internal processes and customer interactions to glean valuable information in the course of daily business. For instance, the highly innovative company 3M makes knowledge creation, which is one step beyond simply generating information, a regular part of its employee process. Employees are encouraged to spend up to 15 percent of their work time on new,

Table 5.2   Seven Modes of Information Generation

Mode of Information Generation	Description	Examples
Acquisition	Information is bought, rented, or borrowed from outside the organization.	• IBM's purchase of Lotus Development Corporation for its knowledge of Notes and collaboration technologies. • Hiring a consultant for a project. • TI's "Not Invented Here but I Did It Anyway" award for borrowing a practice from someplace else.
Dedicated resources	Information is generated by established groups, whose job it is to create knowledge.	Xerox PARC and other internal research and development groups.
Fusion	Information is generated by bringing together people with different perspectives to purposefully generate creative tension.	Nissan Design International's practice of hiring and promoting people with nontraditional backgrounds to create a diverse culture, which encourages discussions of different ideas.
Adaptation	Information is generated as a result of identified changes in the environment and modifications to the organization as a response to the environment.	Lucent Technologies, a spin-off from AT&T, learned how to market products to complement its R&D capability when it became an independent company.

(continued)

85

Table 5.2   *(Continued)*

Mode of Information Generation	Description	Examples
Knowledge networking	Information is generated by informal, self-organizing groups of people with a common interest, goal, or environment.	Society for Information Management's (SIM) symposia, which provide a Web site for members, and has spawned a number of relationships among information systems professionals worldwide.
Internal processes	Information is generated as an output of the processes done as a regular part of the business.	Diamond Technology Partners consulting firm's use of Lotus Notes at the core of its consulting process, which allows the firm to capture knowledge as it is generated and used for clients.
Customer interactions	Information is generated from direct contact by customers.	Fisher-Price's link on its Web site for comments and suggestions, which gives the company information directly from current and potential customers.

Source: Inspired by T. Davenport and L. Prusak. 1998. *Working Knowledge.* Boston: HBS Press.

creative ideas that interest them. Employees spend this time learning new skills, researching new ideas, and developing new processes, all of which result in extremely valuable knowledge creation for 3M. The company ensures the success of this program with a rule: At least 50 percent of its current profits must come from products introduced in the past four years. By embedding knowledge creation into its internal processes, 3M ensures timely and regular creation of usable knowledge.

Instant Learning automatically delivers the right information at the right time, shrinking the learning curve to zero.

Instant Learning companies generate information purposefully and, when possible, automatically. For example, just as 3M deliberately builds knowledge creation into its employee process, Nissan Design International purposefully assembles two-person design teams, whose members come from different backgrounds. This frequently creates an atmosphere of creative tension. Nissan reasons that new information and ideas will emerge from dissonant but creative discussions between the two team members. Information generation is an automatic output of Nissan's internal process, which deliberately creates tension.[7]

Armed with technological advancements, Instant Learning companies generate information regularly, automatically, subtly, and precisely. Fisher-Price, for one, pulls information from customer interactions automatically, inviting customers to send comments, questions, and feedback via its corporate Web site. Amazon.com takes it one step further, automatically gathering data on customer preferences without requiring the customer to initiate the action. For instance, amazon.com automatically develops customer trend data based on customer browsing patterns, analyzing which books customers considered but did not buy, which books customers did buy, and which books customers never even looked at. The next time a customer visits amazon.com's Web site, the system is able to present options consistent with that customer's previous choices, such as offering books similar to those purchased on the customer's last visit.

Unfortunately, unlike the knowledge generated by 3M's employee policy, most information collected in this initial stage of knowledge management is not immediately valuable. Instant Learning companies must first codify the information into a usable system for easy access.

Codify Information Automatically for Immediate Access

Codification is the process of capturing, formatting, and labeling information to make it available to others. Like a puzzle with many pieces, the information nuggets are not valuable by themselves. They become valuable when combined with other nuggets into a cohesive picture that may suggest the launch of new products, substantially cut costs, or identify new markets. Instant Learning companies are experts at this, and they handle this process automatically.

Codification is needed because these companies collect information from such a broad base of sources that the collected information lacks uniformity. Some information is random data, which must be sorted, labeled, and categorized even before it can be evaluated for usefulness. Other information is more organized, but still must be contextualized to become usable. Instant Learning companies use codification to convert all data into information, and sort, format, label, and organize all information into a unified system that is easily accessible.

Microsoft's Product Improvement Team, for instance, as described by Bill Gates, collects, sorts, and analyzes a stunning 7 to 8 million pieces of customer data that pours in over the phone lines, the Internet, and other sources annually.[8] Customer service agents automatically enter customer complaints and problems into the database when they respond to customer input. Microsoft's information system files the service requests and other problems raised from customer interactions into a database, making the information immediately available to the Product Improvement Team.

In addition, the Product Improvement Team collects customer suggestions and comments through the Microsoft Web site, which automatically logs them in to the knowledge management system's database upon receipt. Microsoft receives about 10,000 suggestions for new product features each month by Web, e-mail, fax, and snail-mail. It is the job of the Product Improvement Team to analyze the aggregated data and develop a prioritized list for bug fixes, patches, enhancements, and improvements. This list is then passed on to development teams. The whole cycle happens so fast that the development team is often able to include new features in the next release of their product.

For example, in July 1997, when Microsoft released Internet Explorer 4.0, the Product Improvement Team's codification process resulted in happier customers and decreased support costs. Because of Microsoft's effectiveness at codification, it was able to ship a minor upgrade with features and bug fixes addressing 6 of the top 10 customer complaints within two short months. Just as important, customer support calls for the product decreased by an impressive 20 percent. By leveraging database technology to automatically sort and codify customer feedback data into easily accessible, useful information, Microsoft closed the learning gap and delivered rapid, if not instant, gratification to customers.

To deliver instant gratification to customers,
Instant Learning companies must be able to pull
the right piece of information at the right time,
resulting in value for the customer.

Instant Learning companies take their time and spend the resources required to develop effective codification systems that *simplify* and *automate* the knowledge management process. Similarly, these companies devote resources and focus to the actual conversion of information into knowledge, the critical last phase of knowledge management that yields actual customer value.

Convert Information to Valuable Knowledge

This step of the knowledge management process is crucial, for useful information is converted into indispensable chunks of knowledge that directly help the company provide valued products and services to the customer. Generally, information becomes valuable when enabled to provide instant gratification to customers. Instant Learning companies painstakingly develop their processes to automatically convert information to value at the appropriate moment.

Southwestern Bell, for example, stores reams of customer information in its customer database. The information does not become valuable until the company uses it to satisfy customer demands. To make use of the information and convert it to value, the company has designed its processes and information systems to provide the exact piece of needed information at the appropriate moment. When Southwestern Bell's phone system receives an incoming customer call, it automatically retrieves the caller's number, matches the number with the customer's record from the database, and delivers both call and record to the customer service agent. This gives the agent immediate access to the customer's bill, payment history, service options, and demographics when responding to the call. As the agent uses the information to service the customer request, it becomes valuable because it directly impacts the customer's perception of the service delivered by Southwestern Bell.

Instant Learning companies also use automatic interactions with customers, which do not involve direct involvement from customers, to convert information to knowledge. Internet companies like eToys, amazon.com, and Travelocity carefully manage their Web sites to ensure that customers can instantly access the knowledge they need, rather than have to sort through volumes of information to locate a single knowledge nugget. Such companies place "cookie" files, containing pertinent customer information, on the customer machine, and retrieve and use the file each time the customer visits the site.

During a repeat visit at amazon.com, for example, the interface inquires whether the customer would like to see products similar to those he or she purchased at last visit or search for a new category of products. Amazon.com's entire Internet process guides the user, step by step, to the exact piece of desired knowledge. The information amazon.com stored when the customer last visited amazon.com's Web site, is immediately and automatically converted to value as the system uses it to guide the user to the appropriate product.

Knowledge management is the foundation for
Instant Learning companies, providing the
actual knowledge nuggets that produces
instant customer gratification through
excellent service and high value products.

To deliver instant gratification to customers, Instant Learning companies must be able to pull the right piece of information at the right time, resulting in value for the customer. In these top companies, the response is both automatic and immediate. A key driver of that immediate response is the set of business processes that deliver the knowledge. As with the Southwestern Bell example, relevant information is automatically delivered through the process whereby the representative answers a customer call for service. The information is stored based on the process in which it will be used.

Push the Right Knowledge at the Right Time

Because companies are relentlessly bombarded by waves of information, the temptation is to study the information and decide how to use it. Instant Learning companies resist this temptation, instead focusing on the process and analyzing the particular information that might be needed at any specific point. The structure of the process dictates the type and timing of knowledge to be pushed.

Toshiba, Dell Computer Corporation, and others have embraced and implemented the "right knowledge, right time" concept on their computer assembly lines. As employees in each cell assemble computers, a screen placed in the work cell pushes perfectly timed, step-by-step instructions, tips, and advice out to them. To develop such timely, appropriate knowledge nuggets, these companies studied the assembly process for possible knowledge gaps where workers might need guidance to perform certain tasks, then developed knowledge nuggets to close those gaps. The resulting system, while continuously being updated to match new computer systems being assembled, keeps the assembly line moving without delay.

This concept can be applied to nonmanufacturing processes as well. Many organizations have built in "context-sensitive" help to information-systems-based processes. Microsoft demonstrates superb understanding of the "right knowledge, right time" concept with its Office suite of products. Each product is equipped with interactive help, which senses various situations and delivers knowledge nuggets appropriately. For instance, in Microsoft Word, the help utility pops open in a small, new window when it senses users typing letters, faxes, memos, or reports, and offers help in the form of tips, templates, and suggestions. Microsoft has even designed several alternative, animated icons to deliver this help. The timing and content of the offered help reflect Microsoft's detailed study of the processes involved in the use of its software.

By investing effort to deliver the right knowledge nuggets at the right time, Instant Learning companies like Toshiba, Dell, and Microsoft maximize their chances for Instant Learning. An obvious key to their success is their dependence on sophisticated technology to monitor the process.

Use Technology to Monitor the Process

One secret to delivering the right knowledge nugget at the right time is to know the appropriate technology to use to monitor the process. Instant Learning companies invest heavily in technology, which enables them to detect when workers or users need assistance.

For instance, Internet-driven companies like eToys design their information systems to guide users through the product-ordering process; these systems sense when help is needed or information is lacking. As users enter their information at checkout time, the system verifies that all required fields are complete and in the correct format. The moment the user clicks the Submit button, the system immediately notifies users of incomplete or incorrect information. The system even checks credit card numbers online, eliminating those that are obviously incorrect and that do not "pass" the checking algorithms. The highlight of the system is that no human intervention is required.

Another company, General Motors, builds so-called smart cars that not only alert the driver of needed maintenance or repairs, but can provide directions to the nearest gas station, automatically call a hotline for help, and various other services. Otis Elevator Company, a manufacturer and service provider of elevators and escalators, offers products with built-in intelligence. When maintenance is necessary, this system automatically contacts Otisline, the company's service operation, and schedules the necessary time with the service technician. The system identifies the service needed, and can alert the repair technician as to which parts to bring.[9]

One secret to delivering the right knowledge nugget at the right time is the use of technology to monitor the process.

Technology automates the monitoring function and reduces strain on human resources that are, even for Instant Learning companies, already stressed by intense customer demands for immediate satisfaction. The one aspect of process guidance that technology cannot handle is updating knowledge nuggets to keep them current.

Conduct a Postmortem to Keep Current

Instant Learning companies perform postmortems on major events or nonroutine processes to keep knowledge current. A consulting company employing one of the authors of this book offers informational conferences for seminars on a regular basis. Each event is staged in a different city or focused on a new topic or aimed at a distinct audience, making each event somewhat nonroutine. The group manager then facilitates a postmortem after each event to add to the corporate knowledge about these types of events. Each aspect of the conference is reviewed, including successes, problems, issues, and thoughts for future conferences. No problem is considered too insignificant to discuss. Unexpected changes in plan are examined, and valuable changes are incorporated into future events. The postmortem becomes a corporate learning event that keeps the knowledge fresh, up to date, and reflective of current customer trends.

Instant Learning companies coordinate these postmortem activities with sophisticated technology to monitor processes and the "right knowledge, right time" concept to deliver seamless process guidance to both workers and customers. The entire knowledge management environment relies on a learning culture to achieve maximum benefit for the organization.

Learning Culture

Many companies dedicate themselves to becoming learning organizations, the concept created and popularized in Peter Senge's book *The Fifth Discipline*.[10] Instant Learning companies focus on Instant Learning. They create countless opportunities for learning, information sharing, feedback, communication, understanding, and knowledge management, all of which ultimately allow them to accumulate preparation time (Figure 5.5). They create feedback loops, where information is circulated, analyzed, and used in every aspect of their business processes. They also make it clear that they believe learning to be a valued component of every aspect of their operation, from hiring individuals who share that belief to providing opportunities throughout the firm for learning.

A learning organization:

- Values and practices a lifelong program of study.

- Believes that no individual team has enough resources to build all the knowledge required for success.

- Shares knowledge among individuals, which leads to increased learning.

- Approaches scarce resources by sharing information among departments, business units, and divisions.

- Seeks answers to new questions by building on knowledge obtained by everyone in the company.

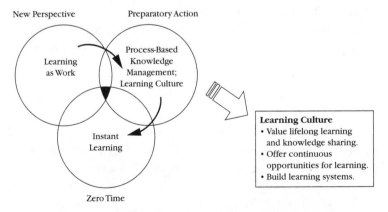

Figure 5.5 Preparatory action: learning culture.

The learning culture in an Instant Learning organization incorporates all of these. Further, the learning culture values speed.

The secret of Instant Learning is in the development
of process and information systems which find,
distribute or update, and push the knowledge
to the worker in a constant stream.

Value Lifelong Learning and Knowledge Sharing

In this section, we address how lifelong learning and knowledge sharing, continuous opportunities for learning, and building learning systems are critical to building Instant Learning. Central to the learning culture is the value of lifelong learning. Instant Learning organizations realize that to continuously satisfy customers and understand their changing preferences, the organization must continuously learn. For the organization to continuously learn, individuals who make up the organization must value lifelong learning.

Valuing lifelong learning means that every individual in the organization must embrace two very profound concepts. First, no one ever knows everything there is to know about any topic. To acknowledge this means letting go of the idea that anyone can have all the answers; this belief precludes the need for additional learning. Second, every event, interaction, and change must be regarded as an opportunity to learn. Viewing everything that happens in the environment as an opportunity to learn something of value is critical to developing the discipline of Instant Learning because gaps are forever emerging, and only those willing to learn from the gaps will be able to close them.

For example, Motorola has made learning a part of its corporate policy. It has a world-class training organization, Motorola University (MU), that complements the training that takes place in each business unit. There are more than 400 professionals on staff, and an additional 700 writers, developers, translators, and instructors involved part-time in 20 offices for MU in 13 countries on 5 continents. In addition, every employee is required to take at least 40 hours of job-relevant training every year. Motorola's annual report summarized its learning philosophy as follows:

The skills of its people are Motorola's most valuable assets. To remain a leader, a technology company needs to renew itself continuously. Its people need to have the knowledge and confidence to lead that change. Motorola University acts as one of the agents of change and enables every employee throughout the world to receive at least one week of training each year.[11]

Offer Continuous Opportunities for Learning

Instant Learning organizations offer multiple opportunities for their workers to learn. We have already discussed Instant Learning, where learning is embedded into the business processes, and Just-in-Time learning, where workers can access knowledge bases on an as-needed basis. But most organizations also offer traditional training classes to employees to help get them up to speed on particular topics.

Traditional training offers significant benefit when appropriately used. Formal classes allow employees to take a break from their daily work environment and concentrate on learning a new topic with a group of like-minded, similarly motivated peers. The interaction with peers also serves to highlight relevant issues and promote productive discussions on the topic. In addition, traditional classes can provide a quick boost of motivation and an infusion of new knowledge and techniques to keep the company moving in creative new directions. Offering excellent training classes can signal the cultural value of learning.

For example, successful clothing retailer The Limited, Inc. clearly values well-trained, adaptable employees. The Limited has devised numerous adventurous and humorous ways to train its employees to use the available knowledge. The company often runs classes with catchy titles like "Retail Math/Retail Speak" for store and merchandise planners to learn basic retailing concepts. Trainees play games like "Let's Make a Deal," to familiarize themselves with retailing concepts, "Lingo Bingo," to learn relevant buzzwords, and "Jeopardy," to test their knowledge of financial metrics. Beth Thomas, training group director for The Limited, explains:

> *People hate generic training. But they don't hate training that's fun, that's relevant to them, and that's rooted in a deep understanding of our business. And that kind of training is good for our business too. It takes less than 2 percent increase in productivity to generate 100 percent return on an investment in training.*[12]

Training classes are kept short, and the presentation of topics is concentrated and fun. About 500 to 1,000 employees per month attend one of 70 courses on topics such as the basics of retailing or the use of business-critical applications. Thomas adds, "The no-show rate is somewhere between 3 percent and 5 percent. That is an outstanding level of attendance. At my previous company, classes were not as large and the no-show rate was 30 percent to 50 percent."

Traditional training classes are not, however, the best way to bridge learning gaps on a continuous basis, because they require workers to stop doing their business tasks in order to attend the class. The basic disadvantages of this type of learning are:

- Pulls employees away from work, resulting in loss of productivity.
- Traditional classroom settings are often less effective learning environments.
- Possible time lag between learning and use may cause students to forget the material.
- Time lag between when the course is developed and delivered, can make the information out of date in a dynamic environment.

Because most companies can barely keep pace with changing customer demands, human resources are already stretched to the limit. Asking workers to take even four hours away from work can be frustrating for them, and result in loss of productivity for the company.

Despite the drawbacks of traditional learning, there appears to be an increasing demand for these types of courses. To minimize the disadvantages and maximize the advantages, Instant Learning companies promoting this type of learning comprehensively redesign their training programs to enhance rapid absorption of new material: The duration of classes is dramatically reduced; new material is delivered in small chunks, which are easy for students to digest; and topics are kept focused and relevant to ensure applicability.

In response to the demand for this type of learning, most business schools, consulting firms, and many private companies offer targeted executive courses to rapidly train executives in the use of the latest business tools and techniques. For example, Career Track, a private training organization, caters to the need for rapid learning by regularly offering eight-hour short courses on relevant management topics including "Dealing with Difficult Individuals," "Providing Motivation and Rewards to Employees," and "Controlling Your Emotions in the Workplace." Career Track holds these seminars off-site, usually at a hotel or conference center in a major metropolitan area, to give students a break from their daily work routine. The company delivers a series of short, intensive workshops on the topic; regular breaks are scheduled to allow students to absorb the material. Though employees must be away from the office for an entire day, they come away with a broad, long-term understanding of the topic.

Offering traditional training classes is one way to begin to establish a learning culture. But it is not enough. All organizational systems must become learning systems. That means that learning must be infused to all activities within the firm. One way to do that is to build learning systems.

Build Learning Systems

In the learning culture, all systems are designed with learning in mind. They systematically support learning, and they, themselves, learn. We call these *learning systems.* Learning systems are organizational or technological systems that have learning components embedded within them. Learning systems have five characteristics, summarized in Table 5.3.

Self-monitoring systems detect problems and exceptions and alert the organization long before problems become system failures. In some cases, self-monitoring systems capabilities extend to self-diagnostics and self-maintenance.

Self-explanatory systems have simple, familiar interfaces that enable users to become immediately proficient. The toolbars in most Windows applications are examples; they all possess similar interfaces, features, and help utilities.

Self-helping systems provide help to users without human intervention. Many Internet-driven companies use Frequently Asked Questions (FAQs) as a way to circumvent the need for worker intervention. The help bubbles in Microsoft's Windows operating system and pop-up assistant in the Office suite of products are good examples.

Self-learning systems improve their capabilities by learning from experience and interactions. For instance, search engines offer helpful tips or additional keywords based on analysis of searches made by past users using similar words.

Table 5.3   Characteristics of the Instant Learning System

System Characteristic	Description
Self-monitoring	System senses, tracks, and fixes or sends out call for help before malfunctioning.
Self-explanatory	System is easy to use and has an intuitive interface, which requires little or no explanation, so user is immediately productive.
Self-helping	System has built-in help and assistance and displays that are available when the user needs them. This help is friendly, understandable, and correctly anticipates the aid needed.
Self-learning	System learns from how it is used, then enhances its search capabilities and knowledge base with this new information.
Self-enforcing	System does not let a user proceed until a fundamental lesson has been mastered.

The system learns what possible right answers are from historical data of searches made on similar words.

Self-enforcing systems ensure that users have fully learned the current topic before allowing them to access another topic. Forms that prevent the user from continuing when a field is improperly completed is an example. In addition, many Just-in-Time learning systems quiz users upon completion of the lesson, and lead the user to additional lessons if the user fails the quiz.

Learning systems support the learning culture. The systems themselves are vehicles for training individuals within

---

All organizational systems must become
learning systems. That means that learning must
be infused to all activities within the firm.

---

the organization because they provide answers and enforce proficiency in the knowledge *before* allowing users to complete the tasks of the system. In this way, workers learn by reinforcement provided by the system. Second, learning systems themselves learn. When the system is used to assist in decision making or another ambiguous task, the system learns how the user addressed the issue; the next time the system is used, it incorporates its previous experience into its response.

Close the Learning Gaps

To respond in Zero Time, the organization must learn instantly. At the core of this discipline is simultaneous proficiency in three areas: knowledge management, learning culture, and training. In a traditional company, a knowledge management group manages the knowledge base, while a training group prepares training courses. Knowledge management is the function of the information systems group or of a separate knowledge organization. Some companies even have chief knowledge officers.

Unfortunately, the typical knowledge management group does not control the training activities; these are usually handled by the human resource group. As a result, learning gaps occur when information gathered by the knowledge management group is not reliably transferred to the training group. Information stored in the knowledge base is the foundation for operational tasks to be performed by workers. How can

---

Instant Learning is the key that enables elite companies to absorb the impact of seemingly endless changes in their industry, while remaining organized, focused, and innovative.

---

learning take place instantly when the knowledge base and the training activities are managed separately? They can't. Therefore, integrating these areas is the essence of the discipline of Instant Learning. Organizationally, that may mean that the chief knowledge officer and the chief learning officer are the same person. It may mean that training is no longer a human resource function, but a knowledge management function, or vice versa. The Instant Learning company understands the value in managing knowledge and learning together.

Instant Learning companies close the gaps by combining work and learning. Employees learn instantly as part of their work. The secret is in the development of process and information systems, which find, distribute or update, and push the knowledge to the worker in a constant stream. Instant Learning companies create this dynamic flow of knowledge throughout the organization. They also recognize that the ultimate key to Instant Learning is not in simply training workers to use knowledge to produce high-value products and services; workers are the ultimate point of contact with customers and, without workers, the most effective and efficient processes to translate and push knowledge are of little value. Therefore, Instant Learning companies build learning into every aspect of the business process, so workers can make use of it with minimal disruption to their work routine. These companies build learning systems.

To keep up with the frantic pace of change in the marketplace, companies will have to focus on Instant Learning as a primary learning modality, while continuing to offer traditional opportunities for learning, including Just-in-Time and classroom training. Instant Learning is the key that enables elite companies to absorb the impact of seemingly endless changes in their industry, while remaining organized, focused, and innovative. Instant Learning is part of the foundation that transforms ordinary companies into Instant Learning companies, in which an endless stream of information flows through the organization and is instantaneously absorbed and transformed into correct action. Without the immediacy of Instant Learning, companies will be hopelessly overwhelmed by the tidal waves of data constantly sweeping over them.

Building an effective learning infrastructure requires detailed preplanning and Instant Learning companies, forever casting their gaze into the future, are masters of preparation and planning.

Dell Computer Corporation: An Instant Learning Company

MANY KNOW THE STORY OF MICHAEL DELL, OF HIS COLLEGE-BASED business of building personal computers with available parts, and of his build-to-order strategy. Founded in 1984 as PCs

The authors would like to thank the managers and executives at Dell Computer Corporation for their contribution to this case, including (listed alphabetically) John Coné, Michael Dell, Scott Eckert, Andy Greenawalt, Jerry Gregoire, Terry Hill, Darcy Kurtz, Keith Maxwell, Paul McKinnon, Tom Meredith, Michelle Moore, Deborah Powell, and Kevin Rollins.

Limited, the name was officially changed worldwide to Dell Computer Corporation when the first stock offering took place, in June 1988. In 1986, when Dell first went outside the United States to Europe, it hit the $50 million mark in sales; and in 1989, the company went from last to first place in the industry in the management of its inventory. In 1993, the concept of segmenting took shape, enabling Dell management to provide better service to its customers. And by 1999, Dell employed more than 12,000 employees in central Texas, its largest workforce, and was in the process of expanding its European facility, in Limerick, Ireland, to 4,500 employees. At the time of this writing, Dell had five plants: three in Texas, one in Ireland, one in Maylasia. A sixth plant was planned for China, and a seventh for Brazil.

At the core of Dell's business is the build-to-order strategy. Customers order PCs directly; their orders are routed through a credit check, then go directly to the manufacturing floor. The computers are built, tested, and shipped to the customers, who receive them within five to seven days of placing their order. Using this model for manufacturing has turned Dell into one of the top computer manufacturers in the world.

Dell Learning is the secret weapon that is transforming Dell Computer Corporation into an Instant Learning company.

The Dell Direct Model is central to all of the Dell management principles; it is the most practical and important principle at Dell because it aligns all of Dell's business units and people. Within the Dell organization, the Direct Model means that everyone is a customer. For example, the IT organization has relatively few central staff; most of the IT personnel report directly to business units. The philosophy of *central planning with local implementation* supports the Direct

Model principle. This philosophy enables the organization to grow at its breathtaking rate because it provides the capability of *build-to-order* for all parts of the organization and all business processes needed to run the corporation.

Dell Learning

Dell Learning, part of the corporate group at Dell Computer Corporation, began in July 1995 as Dell University (Dell U), a virtual university when John Coné, Dell Learning's vice president, internally published Dell's educational philosophy of a commitment to lifelong learning. During Dell Learning's humble beginnings, there was little support. The Dell environment lacked the organizational infrastructure to support learning, expertise for online training, and financial ownership by the business units. Nevertheless, four priorities were outlined to guide the development of Dell Learning. Dell Learning would provide:

- Education required for survival of the company/department.
- Education required for the survival of the individual.
- Education that will take the company/department to the next level of competence.
- Education that will take the individual to the next level of competence.

By July 1999, however, the Dell Web site boasted: "Dell is one of the world's fastest-growing computer companies. Our success depends on what we know, what we learn, and how quickly to apply it. And that's where Dell University (Dell U) comes in. Dell U makes learning easier, simpler, faster." Dell Learning is composed of two branches, a corporate branch, which functions as a service organization for regional training groups, and a regional branch, which acts as an umbrella organization for regional training groups. The corporate organization develops, administers, and maintains an array of training resources because of its centralized expertise and resources. This group offers multiple services, including:

- Assisting the business units in addressing all learning and performance needs.
- Identifying, developing, and implementing technology-enabled learning solutions to reduce classroom hours.
- Managing courses, including registration, administration, and evaluation.
- Supporting Dell business units outside the United States by distributing training materials.
- New product, program management, and regional operations training in both classroom and nonclassroom modes.

Regional training groups, unlike the centralized corporate training organization, belong to the regional business units. Regional training groups have the following objectives:

- Plan the learning needs for business units.
- Obtain necessary training resources to support the plan.
- Hold business leaders accountable for executing the plan.
- Measure the impact of the learning plan.

The corporate group operates on a zero-based budget. Unlike traditional corporate structures, which pay for training as a portion of corporate overhead, Dell Learning's expenses are paid in full by the business units, which allocate funds to develop specific training programs tailored to individual units. These training programs are offered directly to the business unit that requested them, although other units may request the same course once it has been developed. Alternately, business units may collaborate on training programs to share costs and resources. As a result, the menu of training programs is driven by the needs of the business units rather than by guesswork at Dell Learning, and the rate of attendance is high. One training manager explains:

> *In the past, we, like most of our counterparts in other companies, offered classes we thought were needed. We based our offerings on conversations with business managers and executives, and then developed the course. But we, like most of our counterparts in other companies, had a large number of "no-shows." This occurred basically because there was no penalty to the business; or, in the few cases where the manager was charged, it was a relatively small cost compared to their department's overall budget. So now we don't develop or even offer a course without someone in the business paying for it. If it is needed, and someone is willing to pay for it, we gladly make it happen.*

One exception to this approach of allowing business units to drive course development is the series of courses called Red Threads. Red Threads are programs so critical to Dell's business that the corporate organization actually drives the development, implementation, and integration across all business units. In fact, Dell Learning has dedicated corporate and regional staff members whose sole function is to ensure the comprehensive delivery of these courses. Examples of Red Threads program topics include new product training and management development.

Dell Learning's basic strategy is
"learning is synchronous with work."

While most of Dell Learning's classes are offered in-house, only 5 percent to 10 percent of them are developed internally. Dell Learning outsources most classes to external contractors and vendors, including classroom instructors, instructional design experts, Web development resources, and course development companies. Dell Learning often selects standard classes offered by external vendors, who tailor the programs to fit the company's specific needs.

Acting in Zero Time: Dell Delivers Instant Learning

When Dell Learning develops training programs, courses, and techniques, the focus is on Instant Learning. Corporate documents describe this basic strategy as "learning is synchronous with work." Both corporate and regional organizations design formal and informal training programs so that learning is delivered to workers as they do their jobs. John Coné describes Instant Learning at Dell:

> *The ideal "learning event" at Dell has a class size of 1, lasts 5 to 10 minutes, and takes place within 10 minutes of when someone recognizes that he or she needs to know something. Our challenge is to reduce learning to its smallest, most-useful increments and to put the learner in charge of the entire process.*[1]

Instant Learning takes place frequently at Dell. For example, instant, or "stealth" learning occurs on the production line in the manufacturing facility at Metric 12, a plant located in Austin, Texas. As the production line assembler receives a kit to put together, the information system reads the bar code on the kit, determines the type of kit, and "pushes" instructions and guidance specific to that particular kit out to the worker on a computer screen in the station. The guidance is passively available to the worker if needed, which means the worker is not required to actively seek assistance from a traditional learning or JIT system. More important, as errors are uncovered during the test phase of the production line, an entry is made to a networked computer, which is immediately sent to all testers as well as to the individual who assembled the system. In this way, the individual "learns" what he or she did wrong and can immediately correct it. The other lines are also alerted to the problem, to learn mistakes to avoid.

In another area of Dell Learning, Terry Hill, regional training manager for Dell's Large Customer Account Sales organization, also focuses on providing Instant Learning for her business unit. She describes her work:

We are out there in the Dell business functions to pull in resources to do education planning, resource planning, execution, and impact measurements. I need to be proactive in helping my group with their learning needs. It can cost us $70,000 to $100,000 a day in lost sales if I pull people out of the field. Therefore, I spend a lot of my time working with them as a sort of coach while they are doing their job. I provide guidance, skills training, and sometimes organizational knowledge to the sales force as they are doing their jobs. And we see improvements in the way these people perform. Someone I've trained may make more margins on their sales because they know how to sell the services we offer. That is bottom-line impact.

Terry Hill provided Instant Learning to her business unit when she helped business leaders of the Large Customer Account Sales organization develop an implementation plan to meet the fiscal year 2000 strategic plan. As a first step, Hill met with a sales manager in the organization to discuss and define the opportunities to help the field force succeed in implementing the plan. At a national sales meeting, Hill reviewed and clarified the plan for the gathered business leaders. She engaged them in an active discussion to design solutions for meeting the goals of the plan.

To ensure that learning was instant and that successful solutions were devised, Hill facilitated the discussion and ensured that all leaders were involved. In addition, she guided them in designing and implementing an assessment strategy. As a final step, Hill coached the business leaders on how to communicate their plan most effectively. To deliver Instant Learning, Hill assumed the roles of coach, facilitator, trainer, and consultant, offering every required resource to help her group learn even as they completed their tasks. "Training is a process, not an event," she says, "so I get right in there and help them do their business."

New Perspective: Learning as Part of Work

Dell Learning is the secret weapon that is transforming Dell Computer Corporation into an Instant Learning company. Coné, describes the new way of seeing:

> *The teaching philosophy of most companies today is similar to that of the schools I went to. Lots of people sitting in a classroom, with an expert up front telling you things. I've always thought that if that was the natural way for people to learn, we ought to see four-year-olds on the playground spontaneously forming themselves into rows. The natural way to learn is simply to be who we are and to do what we do. Kids learn by doing things. And they learn new things when they need to know them.*[2]

This unique perspective of "throwaway" courses has enabled Dell Learning, which provides both formal and informal training, to respond to the training demands of a fast growth company like Dell. But that is only part of the story. Coné explains:

We are not trying to build systems from soup to nuts. We are only trying to deliver what is needed today and tomorrow. The reason for that is because the learning tools we are creating now must be disposable. We need them right now and they may be thrown away in a few months. By then, we will most likely need to teach something different.

By seeing learning as synchronous with work, Dell Learning has been able to act differently from many other corporate universities or training organizations. It has invested in building process-based knowledge delivery systems that link with corporate knowledge management systems. It has also built a learning culture where education is clearly valued and rewarded.

Preparatory Action: Use Process-Based Knowledge Management, Learning Culture

Process-based knowledge management is a key initiative within Dell, and the company approaches this initiative on two fronts: technology and process-driven learning. On the technology front, many business units within the company are spearheading the development of specific systems to store the information used, requested, or developed as a part of daily work.

Manage Knowledge

Dell Learning is working on its knowledge management system. The goal is to gather, codify, and deliver information to Dell workers with minimal disruption.

Ideally, it would function through e-mail. Workers needing help would simply send questions through normal e-mail channels to the knowledge management system. If the question has been asked before, the knowledge management system would return the entire question, answer, and discussion, stored in the system from previous requests, to the worker. If there is no match for the question in its database, the knowledge management system would parse the question to identify keywords. The system would then search its database for the appropriate "company experts" and forward the question to five or six experts to answer. Any and all experts may answer the question by sending a reply back to the knowledge management system, not the originator of the inquiry. The knowledge management system would compile a digest of all the answers and send the entire discussion back to the originating worker, and store a copy of the discussion for future use in its database. In this way, the knowledge management system—and Dell—learn with continued interaction and experience.

Dell Learning is not afraid to step out of the box
and offer highly untraditional learning options.

Building the knowledge base in this way has several advantages. First, current company experts are clearly identified for anyone seeking specific types of expertise. Second, the system gathers data unobtrusively simply by intercepting the ever present stream of e-mail discussion and by storing the information in an easily accessible format. This saves experts from having to perform the tedious, resource-consuming task of manually populating the knowledge management system with content. Third, the system manages all communications, so that experts and workers alike need only remember the system e-mail address to ask questions or send answers. Fourth, workers have instant access to experts through the system, since the system informs the worker of the names of experts who will receive their question and the names of experts who have sent replies. This enables workers to pursue further contact with particular experts if necessary.

Dell began piloting and testing this type of a system developed by a third-party vendor in 1999, and the system showed great promise in building knowledge management as an enhancement, rather than a disruption, to daily work. But the vendor was taken over by another company, which pulled the product from the marketplace for competitive reasons. Dell is still looking for a system that will allow it to integrate knowledge management directly into its daily business processes, a requirement for Instant Learning companies.

Use Process-Driven Learning

To integrate training seamlessly with business unit objectives, the development of Dell Learning's training programs is guided by the company's core business process. For instance, education planning is always focused to meet defined business objectives, and the resulting business training plans are published on the Web for all to review and to provide input. In addition, in the "pay as you go" training model, for which business units fund and direct the development of training programs, the business unit objectives are automatically included in the training courses. Finally, the regional training managers meet regularly to exchange information and coordinate training efforts across the corporation. Dell Learning has ensured that the corporation's key business processes influence the direction and development of training programs.

"We are not trying to build systems from soup to nuts. We are only trying to deliver what is needed today and tomorrow."

—John Coné

One way Dell Learning keeps training courses aligned with core business processes is through its comprehensive and inclusive new course development method. New courses are often created when the regional training manager meets with a Dell Learning Solutions consultant to assess the business need. The consultant forms a project team, which includes the regional training manager, Dell Learning Technology staff, business subject matter experts, and other appropriate individuals. This inclusive planning method allows experts involved in all relevant business processes to influence the content and delivery of the new course. (See Chapter 11, Closing Inclusion Gaps: Instant Involvement, and Chapter 7, Closing Management Gaps: Instant Adaptation for details on the concepts of inclusion and empowerment.)

Because of Dell's rigorous course development methodology, training programs are "tall," meaning they are designed to have a high impact on the specific business unit requesting the course. A side effect of tall courses is that Dell Learning is less concerned with courses being reusable by other areas of the company. For instance, a course developed for managers in the Finance function is tailored to meet the needs of those managers in that function. However, the same course may be poorly designed for managers in other functions, who operate under differing conditions and circumstances. Dell Learning courses are developed for single use by the business unit funding the course, and can be either discarded after use or retro-fit by other business units to meet their needs.

Learning is managed as a "federation" at Dell, with regional training managers dedicated to educational opportunities within their business units. Regional training managers, whose salaries are paid by business unit managers, align their efforts with business unit objectives. At the same time, regional training managers work together as a team to help Dell Learning corporate develop Red Threads courses. This federation approach results in the development of effective courses driven by business unit objectives, and efficient training delivered by a centralized corporate training arm.

Build a Learning Culture

Part of the success of Dell Learning is the learning culture of Dell Computer Corporation. For the corporation, practicing the discipline of Instant Learning often means delivering training in nontraditional formats. To close learning gaps, Dell has invested in developing a widespread learning culture and technology-driven training techniques, both of which place learning in the path of the workers as they perform their daily work. For an Instant Learning company like Dell, on-the-job training takes on a whole new dimension. For instance, the process for orienting new hires sets the tone for a learning culture. Paul McKinnon, VP of Human Resources, describes:

> *At Dell, 75 percent of the training budget is spent on new hires, job basics, and new product training, and the rest is used for everything else. We send new hires as much information as possible ahead of time. We send them a video tape as well as a list of locations on the Web they can use to get oriented. For executives, as soon as they join Dell, we send them a laptop loaded with a CD providing an overview of Dell, which also has Web addresses for information. This provides a virtual guided tour of Dell even before the executive starts work.*

Dell's widespread learning culture is a direct extension of the Dell Business Model, whose slogan, "be direct," drives an organizational culture in which employees are encouraged toward self-direction. Dell employees often take the initiative to seek out information, expertise, or training as needed. Workers are inculcated with the attitude, "It's my job to go find out." This attitude lends tremendous support to the efforts of the training organization to provide Instant Learning.

Workers are inculcated with the attitude,
"It's my job to go find out."

In addition to benefiting from the "be direct" organizational culture, Dell Learning reaps rewards from Dell's purposefully developed online culture, in which all workers are comfortable using the Internet. New hires at Dell are immediately trained to use the corporate intranet to seek information and resources, and all employees are encouraged to master the Internet. Toward that end, Dell Learning created a Web-based program called "Know the Net." Dell employees access the program, which is not mandatory, when convenient. CEO Michael Dell provides enthusiastic support for the course, and employees who complete the course receive a poster of Michael that reads, "MICHAEL SAYS I KNOW THE NET."

To facilitate the online culture, Dell provides every employee with access to an Internet-capable computer. Even workers in manufacturing groups can access computers through computer kiosks scattered throughout their work area. Dell's online culture empowers the company to distribute computer-based training programs with ease, push knowledge nuggets out to workers as needed, and monitor workers to provide help and guidance.

Dell's online computer culture also offers the priceless advantage of speed, since employees work online at a much faster pace then employees in lower-tech companies. The result of this speed is that workers have the latitude to experiment and take risks, even to fail, as long as they correct their errors. Coné explains the benefits of the rapid response online culture:

I can make a decision, be wrong, see the impact, revise my ideas, make a new decision, be wrong again, see the impact, and revise my idea a second time before most managers in traditional companies even see the impact of their first decision. That gives me tremendous advantage.

The most effective learning often occurs through the direct experience of making and correcting mistakes, and Dell's online culture not only encourages such experimentation but also allows for rapid error detection and correction.

The following set of guiding principles contribute to Dell's creation of a learning culture:[3]

- *Strategically centralize.* Establish a critical mass of key skills, and leverage economies of scale.

- *Decentralize.* Place training resources in the business segments.

- *Outsource.* "Buy before we build."

- *Implement pay-as-you-use tuition model.* Businesses own the responsibility for education; learning resides with the learner, not with the teacher/manager; and the marketplace for learning is boundary-less, no longer front-end loaded or time-bound.

- *Provide and implement solid training planning.* Look toward future needs, and have a plan for delivering.

The learning culture at Dell Computer Corporation is supported by organizational and control mechanisms such as rewards, tuition, planning, and systems. All are aligned to support the ability of the corporation's employees to learn, to be innovative, and to make and recover from mistakes, all of which are crucial to the Instant Learning discipline.

How Does Dell Computer Corporation Do It?

Dell Computer Corporation is exemplary in its use of information systems as both the tool for executing processes and

---

A side effect of "tall" courses is that Dell Learning
is less concerned with courses being reusable
by other areas of the company.

---

for delivering learning. Since learning is part of the work itself, the infrastructure becomes a critical component of an Instant Learning company.

Most of Dell Learning's delivery mechanisms involve technology infrastructure. In 1995, 75 percent of the training performed by this organization was delivered in traditional classroom settings, using traditional teaching methods such as lectures and discussions. By 1999, 75 percent of training was delivered in nontraditional formats, including computer-based training over the company intranet or via customized online applications developed to train workers on specific business processes.

For example, new field sales representatives are trained with a self-paced learning kit. According to an article in *Fast Company* in 1998, the field-sales kit comes in a cardboard box labeled, "In-a-box training for out-of-the-box times."[4] Inside, new sales representatives find a videotape on selling Dell products, a CD-ROM with Dell product descriptions, and a video about product benefits that the salesperson will want to relate to his or her customers. The CD-ROM, a snazzy interactive training vehicle filled with games and case studies, has eliminated a staggering 16 hours of classroom time. Sales-training manager Darcy Kurtz describes the benefits of the CD-ROM:

> *We didn't really believe we could replace 16 hours of class time with a tool that took one or two hours and was a lot more fun. But the reps loved it, in part because they could refer back to it easily. And it helped us get them up to speed faster, which meant they started selling sooner.*

Another successful aspect of Dell's learning infrastructure is a set of learning templates that help regional training managers and business managers design and develop Web-based training programs. The learning templates include tools for designing the format of the content of the Web-based program, tools that aid in combining different media, and tools for evaluating how much the student has learned. The templates provide a basis for instantaneously developing training materials that enable managers to construct a training program within minutes. This method of rapidly developing courses makes courses immediately useful and, when no longer needed, disposable. More important, the templates ensure that all Web-based training courses have a consistent interface so that users become immediately proficient.

Dell uses the same infrastructure it set up to help customers as a means of teaching its own workers how to solve problems. The principle of "Dell on Dell" means that its hardware platform for delivering learning through the corporate intranet are composed of Dell servers, and the software platform comprises Windows NT, with Oracle for the database and Microsoft Office for standard business applications. The Dell Client Assistance Center, a help desk, provides technical support for all employees with telecom issues. If the call cannot be resolved in 15 minutes, it is escalated to the technical group that can best help. In that way, employees using the Assistance Center learn how to solve their technical problems, and the Assistance Center's mechanisms build in continuous learning.

Dell Learning demonstrates Instant Learning characteristics with its highly customized, if nontraditional, learning structure and environment. Dell Learning is not afraid to step out of the box and offer highly innovative learning options. For example, Dell Learning turns to such technologies as Video Visor, leading-edge concepts like disposable courses, and incentive structures that force business units to accept responsibility for the funding and development of training courses. Dell Learning eagerly accepted the challenge to reduce 16 hours of classroom learning to a two-hour interactive CD-ROM, and willingly outsources course development needs to outside experts. All of these acts have propelled Dell Learning and, by extension, Dell Computer Corporation, to succeed in implementing the Instant Learning discipline.

Messages for Managers

As the Dell Computer Corporation case illustrates, companies practicing the Instant Learning discipline have shaped themselves into learning organizations with comprehensive knowledge management systems that are optimized for speed. We summarize the key lessons here:

- *Create an environment for learning.* Dell Learning not only supports, but actively promotes learning. The culture has been created to obtain, share, store, and use information. And that culture provides a properly trained workforce, and sparks opportunities for creativity, to generate new types of knowledge. The learning culture thus values learning for more than work tasks. The environment promotes learning for the sake of learning. Employees are encouraged to see the fun in learning and to seek out opportunities to learn.

- *Learn from the past.* Incorporating information from past experiences into planning for future activities means the information must be collected on a timely basis and must be accessible at the time it is needed. One way to collect this information is to subsume the data collection tasks in with regular business tasks, as the Dell Learning knowledge management activities seek to do. Another is to perform postmortems for all situations so that past mistakes and opportunities are documented while fresh. Dell Learning has shown that lessons can be learned from both successes and failures.

- *Reward learning.* Learning from others in the company can be accomplished when rewards are given for teaching others, for sharing information, and for communicating best practices. And if learning is to be successful when it is critically needed, it must be part of the management control and reward systems. At Dell, not only are employees promoted when they demonstrate new skills, but those who helped them advance are rewarded, too.

- *Manage the knowledge life cycle.* To close learning gaps, it is critical to understand and manage every aspect of the knowledge life cycle, to plan for capturing, storing, using, and retiring information, as well as for incorporating it into the learning activities. It is essential to develop easy-to-use information systems and to provide incentives for use, as Dell Learning has done.

- *Develop a comprehensive learning plan that integrates learning activities and knowledge management activities.* Dell Learning has responsibility for building or buying a knowledge management system. That encourages the integration of both knowledge management with training and learning.

7

Closing Management Gaps: Instant Adaptation

THE PACE OF BUSINESS TODAY IS TOO QUICK AND THE GLOBALI-zation of organizations too widespread to accommodate the slow-moving decision making process of traditional corporate hierarchies. Driven by technology and market trends, an elite company must possess a collective intelligence, a deep-seated, almost instinctive ability to make the right decision at the right time in every situation. In this hyper-growth, hyper-change knowledge society, an organization must empower and trust its people, within the bounds of its core purpose, to make decisions and act.

Consider the Killer Bees, a high school basketball team from Bridgehampton, New York, which accumulated a record

125

Table 7.1　The Essence of the Instant Adaptation Discipline

Current practice	People management via empowerment
New perspective	Holonic management
Preparatory action	Constancy of purpose
	Trusting culture

of 163 wins and 32 losses.[1] The team qualified for the state championship playoffs six times, won twice, and finished in the final four two other times. The significance of this team lies not in its outstanding record, but in the fact that the team comes from a small town with a declining population. The Killer Bees' high school has a total enrollment of just 41 students, only 20 of them male, and the team consists of only 7 members, none of whom is extraordinary in talent or ability. John Niles, Killer Bees team coach until 1991, attributed the team's success to the following: "They are committed to bringing honor and recognition to their community, to protecting and enhancing their legacy, and to one another." Each of the seven members of this winning team has assumed leadership responsibility for the success of the entire team, and each player has full knowledge and responsibility to deliver that success. Members of successful companies today claim the same responsibility for the success of their company. We call this the Instant Adaptation discipline, the essence of which is described in Table 7.1.

Current Practice Creates Management Gaps

We have learned from very early times to divide complex problems into smaller components to make them more manageable. For the past 200 years, ever since the Industrial Revolution, we have built organizations and enterprises based on Adam Smith's thesis that work should be divided into its simplest and most basic tasks. Smith's principles and practices, as refined by Frederick W. Taylor, and enhanced by Henry

Ford and Alfred P. Sloan, transformed American industry from craftsmanship to mass production. This transformation brought about an impressive gain in overall productivity.

However, entering the twenty-first century of a postindustrial, global business age, we have come to realize the deficiencies of this kind philosophy for managing an organization as a machine. Such thinking produces gaps. Gaps occur when the organization cannot properly structure itself to perform its functions, as a result of believing that organizations are machines and that people are replaceable cogs in the wheels that turn them. Consequent to this belief is that bureaucracy is created and levels of hierarchy are increased when an organization grows. Bureaucracy not only causes delays, but chokes off communications as well. It encourages people to hoard information rather than share it, which generates mistrust among people.

Bureaucracy not only creates delays, but chokes off communications as well. It encourages people to hoard information rather than share it, and it generates mistrust among people.

Gaps also occur because the organization lacks purpose and vision, as many are primarily concerned with their quarterly financial performance, driven by Wall Street analysts. Similarly, if an organization lacks leadership, it often becomes paralyzed, which also produces gaps.

The current organizational response to bridging these gaps is empowerment, whereby companies grant individuals and teams full responsibility and authority to serve the customer. Unfortunately, without a well-grounded system of ethics and a strong guiding vision, empowerment tends to generate competition rather than collaboration among the various corporate teams and divisions. As each individual team or group takes independent action, the entire company becomes paralyzed by the competing forces.

The Instant Adaptation discipline is about more than just empowering people. It is a whole new way of organizing and working to create instant adaptation.

Acting in Zero Time: Instant Adaptation

Companies that have mastered the Instant Adaptation discipline respond to changes in the business terrain with instinctive speed and mutual cooperation. They respond with the same organic intelligence and native wisdom found in nature. Hence, we turn to examples in nature to illustrate the essence of this discipline.

An Instant Adaptation company operates much like a school of fish, which also adapts instantly to its circumstance. In less than a second, an entire school of fish can simultaneously change direction. When the fish encounter a possible danger in the water, such as a predator, the school often divides into several groups to circumvent the danger. Even though each group is taking an independent path, the entire school is still swimming in the same direction.

An Instant Adaptation company behaves no differently. Each individual or team within the organization, similar to a single fish in the school, takes independent action to deliver value to the customer. At the same time, each group or individual stays focused on the organization's core purpose and vision, which prevents counterproductive action. More important, all the groups are interconnected by bonds of mutual trust and rapid communication. Thus, when a single group detects a change in the business environment, every part of the organization responds appropriately, either to avoid danger or to capitalize on a new opportunity. Like the school of fish, the Instant Adaptation company adapts instantly (see Figure 7.1).

Figure 7.1 Essence of Instant Adaptation.

New Perspective: Manage Holonically

To adapt so rapidly, an Instant Adaptation company must view the organization much differently from the traditional enterprise. It sees that empowerment alone can result in random and chaotic action that is often at cross-purposes to the company's primary aim. Moreover, empowerment often leads to competition. Instead, Instant Adaptation companies look beyond empowerment to a new way of organizing. We call it *holonic management* (see Figure 7.2).

The word holonic was coined by Taro Nawa of NEC, who used the term to describe his vision of NEC in the twenty-first century. He combined the two Greek words *holos,* which means whole, and *on,* which means individual. Nawa described the resulting combination: "Holon is individual. At the same time, it's whole." In other words, a holon is a whole within the whole.

Instant Adaptation companies see the people and teams with their organizations as holons, complete and independent wholes within the whole of the organization. As with empowerment, holonic management gives individuals, groups, or

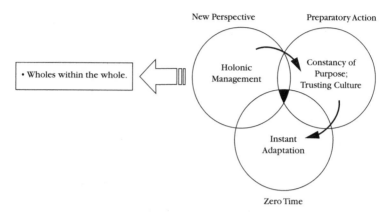

Figure 7.2 Instant Adaptation: new perspective.

teams—all of which are holons—the authority and responsibility to act independently to serve the customer. Unlike empowerment, however, holonic management sets the company's common vision as the highest priority, and gives each holon the necessary knowledge and ethics to fulfill the common vision.

> We have come to realize the deficiencies of the philosophy for managing an organization as a machine.

With holonic management, the company does not give individuals or teams specific instructions on how to act, but it does require them to stay within the boundaries of the company's common vision and ethics. The combination of freedom and boundaries allows each individual to unleash his or her creativity to meet business challenges, while ensuring that these independent actions are well coordinated. In this way, each small part of the organization is a whole, or holon, which has access to all the knowledge, vision, and resources of the entire organization. They are wholes within the whole.

Companies like Toyota put the first steps of holonic management into action in the late 1970s. At Toyota, workers are empowered to stop an assembly line for quality reasons. The company found that workers are the most likely to spot quality problems, and thus gave them the control and responsibility to do so. Another company, Progressive Insurance, has authorized its mobile agents to make instant claims settlements, guided by the company's ethics and business rules.

In a business environment where the terrain changes second by second, the independent, but well-coordinated, freedom of action offered by holonic management is the only way to create instant adaptation.

Preparatory Action: Develop Constancy of Purpose and Build Trusting Culture

The ability to adapt instantly depends on two key core competencies (see Figure 7.3). The first is a constancy of purpose, which constantly guides and directs the organization. The second is a solid foundation of trust between the company and its people, and among the people within the company.

Develop Constancy of Purpose

Constancy of purpose focuses people of diverse backgrounds on a single purpose, which is broad enough to remain constant despite continuous changes in market and corporate conditions. For instance, Sony's co-founder Masaru Ibuka expressed the purpose of incorporation as: "To pursue dynamic activities in technology and production for the reconstruction of Japan and the elevation of the nation's culture." This powerful statement, penned in 1945, was comprehensive enough to focus all stakeholders on growing and expanding

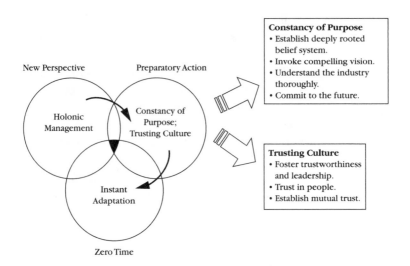

Figure 7.3 Instant Adaptation: preparatory action.

the company, despite the devastation to Japan's economy by World War II. Later, Chairman Akio Morita paraphrased Ibuka in this updated purpose statement: "Sony is a pioneer and never intends to follow others. Through progress, Sony wants to serve the whole world."[2] These words act as an guidepost for Sony employees in their daily work. They provide a constancy of purpose.

A compelling vision is one so irresistible that
it immediately becomes a shared vision.

W. Edwards Deming suggests that "your customers, your suppliers, your employees need your statement of constancy of purpose—your intention to stay in business by providing product and service that will help man live better and which will have a market."[3] The constancy of purpose is much larger, more permanent, more global, and more service-oriented than a company's daily focus on profitability or market share. An Instant Adaptation company's constancy of purpose is its highest choice, which is usually to be of service.

Several key ingredients are required for creating a constancy of purpose: a deep-rooted belief system, a compelling shared vision, and a commitment to the future (see Figure 7.4). Most elite companies possess one or two of these ingredients. Instant Adaptation companies own all three.

Establish Deeply Rooted Belief System

Instant Adaptation companies are anchored by a set of core values, or beliefs, which comprise the acid test against which the appropriateness of any decision is measured. The essence of Instant Adaptation is trust and freedom. Instant Adaptation companies trust their employees with the authority to make decisions on behalf of the entire company, not a responsibility to be granted lightly. To ensure their employees will wield such authority with wisdom, Instant Adaptation companies

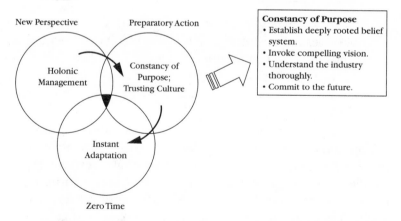

Figure 7.4 Preparatory action: constancy of purpose.

are careful to indoctrinate each new employee in the corporate belief system.

Consider, for instance, the Tylenol incident in 1982, in which seven people in the Chicago area died because someone had tampered with Tylenol bottles and laced the capsules with cyanide. Johnson & Johnson, the maker of Tylenol, immediately pulled all Tylenol bottles from the entire U.S. market at a cost of more than $100 million.[4] Ultimately, by following the core values of the company, Johnson & Johnson made the best decision for all of its stakeholders, including customers, doctors, employees, shareholders, and communities. The benefit of basing decisions on core values is the positive result that follows. Decisions based on core values will always produce results of highest value to all stakeholders. Had Johnson & Johnson failed to recall all Tylenol bottles off the shelves, for fear of angering shareholders because of the enormous cost, the company would have suffered in the long run under the weight of negative public opinion. Thus, the management team's decisive action, grounded in the corporate credo, protected the company's reputation and, as a result, increased the value for shareholders.

Unfortunately, without a well-grounded system of ethics and a strong guiding vision, empowerment tends to crate competition rather than collaboration among the various corporate teams and divisions.

A deeply held belief system fosters trust, allowing Instant Adaptation companies to confidently bestow authority on employees to make independent decisions, take responsibility, handle communications, and act on behalf of the entire organization. Companies lacking such a set of core values are like anchorless boats adrift on the endless sea of change that is today's marketplace.

Invoke a Compelling Vision

When President Kennedy proclaimed in 1961 that "this nation should commit itself to achieving the goal, before this decade is out, of landing a man on the moon, and returning him safely to Earth,"[5] the American people were immediately engaged. So compelling was this vision that scores of people overcame seemingly impossible barriers to achieve this enormous task.

For instance, as Peter Senge reported in *The Fifth Discipline*, MIT's Draper Laboratories, the lead contractor for building the inertial navigational and guidance systems for the moon mission, discovered that after spending millions of dollars, its original design specifications were incorrect. The team was convinced that the development of new specifications was critical to the success of the mission. Rather than hiding their mistakes and finding possible workarounds, the team, at the risk of losing both the contract and their rather significant reputations, suggested to NASA that the design be scrapped and a new one developed. That the team was willing to risk such losses indicates the powerful influence of Kennedy's challenge, his vision of a man on the moon.[6]

Any vision less grand, offered by anyone less captivating than Kennedy, would perhaps lack the force necessary to bring so many people and companies, with such diverse backgrounds and experience, into alignment to produce a successful result. A compelling vision is one so stirring that it immediately becomes a shared vision. In the case of the moon mission, the vision sparked the need of the American people to be first, to win the space race against the Russians, to explore areas unknown, and to demonstrate the might and superiority of the leading nation in the free world.

Elite companies like NEC and IBM have crafted equally compelling visions and have expended major efforts to imbue that vision into the corporate culture. These vision statements have contributed largely to the longevity, and constancy, of these companies. However, a compelling vision statement is hardly enough to create an Instant Adaptation company. These companies need deep insight into their own industries. Neither is a compelling vision the result of off-site corporate retreats. Rather, it is the company's insight into the industry, which reveals that magical intersection of demographics, politics, technology, and lifestyles that produces a new white space in the marketplace.

Understand the Industry Thoroughly

Along with creating a compelling vision for the enterprise, Instant Adaptation companies must also develop a deep understanding of their industries. While many companies develop a basic understanding of the forces that shape their industries, Instant Adaptation companies focus on the peripheral, more subtle, factors, and combine this focus with out-of-box thinking to create new marketplaces. In fact, according to authors G. Hamel and C.K. Prahalad, in their book *Competing for the Future,* "Seeing the future first may be more like a wide-angle lens than a crystal." They cite two examples, which we paraphrase here.[7]

Dr. Edward Land, creator of the Polaroid camera, combined his deep insight into the camera industry with his young daughter's request to see photographs as soon as they were taken. The consideration of instant photography, hardly a major driving force in the industry at the time, combined with Land's ability to immediately see the white space, the need, for such a device, created a new marketplace completely dominated by the Polaroid camera.

Swiss engineer Nicolas Hayek reconceptualized the Swiss watch-making industry with a similar focus on a peripheral force in the industry: cost. The Swiss have always focused on the reliability and quality of its timepieces, never on cost. Hayek asked an almost startlingly simple question: "Why can't we design a striking, low-cost, high-quality watch, and build it in Switzerland?" From that basic question, the SWATCH, the low-cost, popular fashion watch, was born.[8]

An Instant Adaptation company's tireless search for such treasured but hidden marketplaces yields many "aha's" like the Polaroid camera or SWATCH. This relentless intent, no small measure of a company's constancy of purpose, is a defining part of what sets Instant Adaptation companies above companies that are excellent, but not Instant Adaptation.

Commit to the Future

Hesitation is a word rarely, if ever, used to describe Instant Adaptation companies. Once a decision has been made, the entire weight of an Instant Adaptation company is thrown behind it, and the company begins its all-out push toward inevitable success. Instant Adaptation companies make a total commitment to the future they envision.

Instant Adaptation companies make a total commitment to the future they envision.

In 1962, when IBM decided to build System 360, the mainframe computer it envisioned would force all competitive computers such as Burroughs, RCA, Honeywell, Univac, and General Electric into obsolescence, the vision of market dominance was as compelling as the risks were frightening. The 360 strategy would terminate even the usefulness of IBM's own existing computers, thousands of which were already placed in companies, and collecting a high rent. As Bob Evans, team leader of the System 360 project and corporate vice president for engineering and programming in the 1980s, fondly recalls, "IBM bet the company on this project."

The System 360 strategy raised two daunting challenges for the company. IBM not only had to coordinate the hardware and software, which included the never-before encountered task of writing millions of lines of code for the operating system, but also had to manufacture all of the electronic components for the system itself. Years later, Tom Watson, Jr. recalls asking Vin Learson, then overall project manager, to estimate the software budget. Learson replied, "$50 million," despite his answer a few months earlier of "$40 million." Watson later asked the same question of Watts Humphrey, in charge of programming production, and got the answer "$60 million." IBM eventually sank more than $500 million into the development of the System 360 software.

Despite staggering costs and seemingly insurmountable barriers to success, IBM kept its commitment to its vision of the future and went on to dominate the computer industry for more than two decades. Tom Watson, Jr. reflects on his feelings prior to the launch of System 360: "It was the biggest, riskiest decision I ever made, and I agonized about for weeks, but deep down I believed there was nothing IBM couldn't do."[9]

Once the research is complete, once all the factors have been debated and understood, Instant Adaptation companies plunge into the future without pause or hesitation, strengthening their constancy of purpose.

Build Trusting Culture

A trusting culture fosters an ethical organization that binds people with a commonly agreed-upon code of ethics. For instance, in the Tylenol incident mentioned earlier, Johnson & Johnson didn't hesitate to recall all bottles of the painkiller, despite never having encountered a situation of such dire magnitude before. Disregarding the rather staggering cost of the action, the Johnson & Johnson management team acted in accordance with the corporate credo: "We believe that our first responsibility is to the doctors, nurses, hospitals, mothers, and all others who use our products." In times of crisis, as in the Tylenol situation, when panic and blame tend to run rampant, the Johnson & Johnson credo guided the management to the right solution.

Culture shapes the relationships among entities in an organization. In order to facilitate the realization of instant

CUSTOMERization, we believe that the culture of an Instant Adaptation company must be based on trust. There are three kinds of trust important to Instant Adaptation companies: trustworthiness, trust among individuals in a team or organization, and trust between an individual and his or her organization (see Figure 7.5).

Foster Trustworthiness and Leadership

Trustworthiness represents a certain level of self-confidence in an individual's ability to master his or her work and life. An Instant Adaptation organization not only expects its employees to have professional competency, but also fosters a climate that encourages people to create a personal vision and to challenge the status quo. This type of culture requires commitment from both the individual and the organization. The individual must be competent in performing assigned work tasks, while the organization must be committed to supporting each individual to gain the competencies necessary to engender trustworthiness.

Inepar, an energy and telecommunications company with headquarters in Curitiba, Brazil, knows how to enrich people.

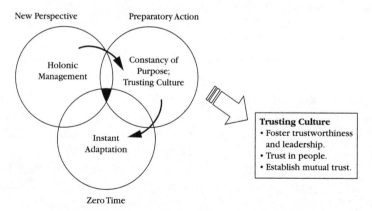

Figure 7.5 Preparatory action: trusting culture.

The company's symbol is a Brazilian bird called Quero Quero, meaning, in Portuguese, "I want, I want." The first "I want" symbolizes the wants of employees, including a better quality of life, a higher salary, professional growth, training, and trust. The second "I want" symbolizes the needs of the company, including total quality, higher productivity, the expansion of business, the incorporation of new technologies, and environmental preservation. Together, the stakeholders find the common "I wants" and work toward achieving these common goals.

Atilano Sobrinho, co-founder and president of the company, is fond of saying, "I learned from the poor people that they don't have a problem with being poor, but having no prospects in life is a big problem." Because Sobrinho wishes to enrich his employees' prospects in life, Inepar pays the educational expenses of every employee's dependent children. Inepar not only commits to enriching its employees, but also its employees' families. In response to this corporate "trust," Inepar's productivity has soared, growing by more than 50 percent from 1992 to 1996, *without* the addition of new employees.

In an Instant Adaptation company, each person accepts the mantle of authority and responsibility for leadership.

An Instant Adaptation organization takes trustworthiness one step further by ensuring that leadership permeates the entire organization. In an Instant Adaptation company, each person accepts the mantle of authority and responsibility for leadership. Nothing less will enable a company to navigate the complex, high-speed, and geographically far-flung digital marketplace. Perhaps the best way to describe the distributed leadership in an Instant Adaptation company is to use a sports analogy: Top managers act as coaches and employees make up the team; coaches work with and prepare the team before competition, but once the game starts, the players must demonstrate their trustworthiness.

Such distributed leadership does not emerge by itself. It takes preparatory time to set up the organizational systems to develop and reward leadership. For example, when Continental Airlines was climbing out of bankruptcy, it rewarded each crew member of every plane that arrived on time with a $65 bonus.[10] Hence, crew members began assuming leadership roles to ensure that planes arrived on time. In Instant Adaptation companies, trustworthiness and leadership are two-way streets; the employees accept greater responsibility for their role in the company, and the company offers opportunities for employees to enrich their skills.

Trust in People

An Instant Adaptation organization always needs to be able to instantly organize itself to adapt to changing business conditions. Such rapid organization is possible only if the people in the company can trust each other to act in the best interests of the company. The trust that members of a sports team must put in each other during the heat of competition is a good analogy for this kind of trust. Before and after the game, players have the leisure to practice their skills and to discuss ways to improve the team's overall performance. During a game, however, players must trust each other to take the appropriate actions that will produce a team win.

In the corporate world, teams must have the same kind of trust. Consider Team Taurus at Ford. In 1980, when Ford, along with GM and Chrysler, lost heavily to the Japanese automakers, Ford decided to replace its Ford LTD model, then targeted at young and middle-aged customers. It was a tactic to attract these customers, who were rapidly shifting loyalties to Toyota, Honda, and Nissan back to Ford. The project was given to Lew Veraldi. At that time, Ford had just begun a series of employee involvement, participatory management, and multi-departmental teaming programs, so Veraldi naturally assembled a team from various departments to serve on the Taurus operating committee.[11]

One of the major contributing factors to the success of the Taurus design was the team's trust in the abilities of the company's employees to create a best-selling vehicle. For instance, the Taurus team asked co-workers to suggest features for the new car, and eventually incorporated over 80 percent of the suggested features into the final design. The team also demonstrated its trust in employees by asking hourly workers in the primary assembly plant to provide design suggestions. The workers responded not only by providing more than 1,400 suggestions, but also by reducing rework from 10 percent to 1 percent and decreasing the cost of last-minute design changes from the usual $150 million to a mere $35 million. Team Taurus demonstrated its trust in Ford employees by asking for suggestions; the employees showed their trust in the team by working hard to make the vehicle a success. The Taurus example demonstrates how companies benefit from the development of trust among its people.

The essence of Instant Adaptation
is trust and freedom.

Instant Adaptation companies also receive numerous secondary benefits from trust among its employees. Perhaps the most significant is the increased sharing of knowledge and information. As trust becomes a shared value in the corporate culture, workers no longer feel the need to hoard information; in an environment of trust, workers no longer need to withhold knowledge as a source of power.

For example, at Intel, the world's largest microprocessor company, technical knowledge sharing is an essential part of the company's culture, and is acknowledged as being the key to gaining speed and competitive advantage. To achieve the goal of "dramatically improving the development process and the ramping of new products to reach the target of achieving volume production with the very first design of a product," Intel's Microprocessor group developed a Web-accessible database of best-known methods, which includes processes, simulation results, circuit design layouts, and postmortems on every project.[12] The program has been a massive success, and the new product ramp time has been accelerated by a factor of almost 2 since 1994. With such benefits, companies practicing the Instant Adaptation discipline, like Intel, are eager to foster trust among employees.

Establish Mutual Trust

Instant Adaptation companies are perhaps the most interested in developing trust between the company and its employees, since this has historically been an area of characterized by lack of loyalty. To create this kind of trust, all managers, employees, and closely linked partners must understand and agree with the corporate direction, and expect all others to come to the same understanding.

Instant Adaptation companies are not shy about crossing traditional organizational boundaries to include both suppliers and customers into their culture of trusting relationships.

Consider the General Motors Fremont, California, manufacturing plant, which has experienced both distrustful and trusting cultures, with widely differing results. In the 1970s, the Fremont plant was often referred to as the "battleship," because of constant warring between management and union leaders. The plant suffered under constant strikes, sickouts, and out-of-control absenteeism. As a consequence, the plant's productivity was in perpetual decline, despite

General Motors spending millions to keep the plant in operation. Finally, in 1982, after the Big Three American automakers suffered unprecedented losses to Japanese competition, General Motors was forced to shut the plant down.

The plant shutdown was temporary, however, as Toyota and General Motors agreed to share a joint venture project using the site in 1983. The new organization, called New United Motor Manufacturing Inc. (NUMMI), built a solid foundation for a trusting culture. NUMMI not only promised to hire many of the previous plant employees, but invited former strike leader Tony DeJesus to aid in evaluating candidates.

The new management emphasized cooperation to diffuse anarchy, and trust to alleviate suspicion. NUMMI promised to apply the same standards to both executives and workers in case of layoffs. In exchange, NUMMI asked the labor union to relax its stringent job classification categories from hundreds to four. This radical reduction in the number of categories allowed the NUMMI to more easily hire workers without waiting for a worker with the "right" classification to appear. As a result of NUMMI's diligent efforts to cultivate trust between the company and its workers, the plant became a model to the auto industry for creating trusting labor-management relations, leading to maximum productivity.[13]

Having developed the three kinds of trust, Instant Adaptation companies are not shy about crossing traditional organizational boundaries to include both suppliers and customers into their culture of trusting relationships.

Consider Xerox. When Xerox established its Personal Products Division in 1992, it was a small player in a market dominated by Japanese companies. By the end of 1996, however, Xerox emerged as the market leader; and shattering traditional organizational boundaries and hierarchies contributed largely to this success. Xerox, like many Instant Adaptation companies, pulls both suppliers and customers into its cross-boundary product design process.

For instance, based on feedback from customers, Xerox approached potential vendors with a modular product that included multiple servicing options, including a self-service repair with 24-hour hotline support. To boost the product's chances of success, the company formed cross-functional teams around core process, from market strategy to product marketing to service deliveries. Finally, Xerox designed the teams to be interlocking, with all teams sharing responsibility for the product's success, and all teams coached by one manager. The manager, by extension, was given total authority to make all decisions necessary to bring the product to market. This unusual organizational structure, combined with multiple points of contact with suppliers and customers, allowed Xerox to move quickly, respond to market conditions, and, eventually, emerge as the market leader.[14]

Xerox's experience provides some clues about the elements of the new organizational structure for instant adaptation (see Figure 7.6):

- Organize teams around core processes rather than around function.
- Invite customers and suppliers to participate in cross-boundary design teams.
- Empower interlocking teams with total authority and shared responsibility.

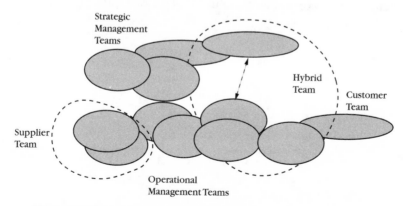

Figure 7.6 Fluid team structure of a Zero Time enterprise.

Close the Management Gaps

Stephen Covey, in his book *Principle-Centered Leadership,* offers some parallels between fishing and managing. In his view, "Senior-level executives are really fishing the stream. That is, they're looking at the business in the context of the total environment and devising ways to reel in the desired results." He elaborates: "Once you see the trends are starting to turn, the trick is to adapt—to make your internal operations harmonious with the external environment."[15]

The boundary conditions for adaptation rest on two foundations: the core beliefs and the vision of an organization. In other words, a successful organization will constantly harmonize its internal and external environments in response to changes in the environment. But these changes are carefully orchestrated to align with the organization's core beliefs and vision, to keep it moving in the direction of its vision (depicted in Figure 7.1). Often, managers study the "stream" through their existing model, their internal environment; hence they are at a loss when the stream, the external environment, changes direction. They no longer know where to look for the fish. The Instant Adaptation discipline shows companies how to think outside of their traditional model and to adapt their internal structure and system instantly to match new external environments. This discipline is all about instant adaptation.

CHAPTER

8

General Electric: An Instant Adaptation Company

THOMAS EDISON FOUNDED GENERAL ELECTRIC (GE) IN 1879 TO fulfill his vision of a company that would light up the nation by providing all the necessary components, from electric power stations to electric lamps. When Jack Welch took over the reins of the company more than a century later, the company had become the eleventh largest corporation in the United States, boasting approximately 440,000 employees, $20 billion worth of assets, revenues of $272.24 billion, and a market value of $12 billion.[1]

Despite these impressive figures, GE was steadily decaying under its façade of public success, hindered by a complex bureaucracy and its legacy. Its nine-layer hierarchy created deep

147

functional boundaries and an inwardly focused culture. Industry pundits degradingly referred to GE as a GNP company, pointing out its low productivity of 1 to 2 percent. GE, previously the crowning glory of American industry, was becoming a slumbering giant.

Undaunted by these inauspicious circumstances, Welch leapt to the challenge, and eventually transformed GE into a lean, agile, global company ready to compete in the information age of the twenty-first century. GE, which now prides itself on speed, simplicity, and boundarylessness, has number-one ranking businesses in 10 world markets, from traditional industrial motors to television broadcasting (with NBC and CNBC). The company's assets and market value have soared to nearly $300 billion on more than $90 billion in sales. In contrast, its number of worldwide employees has shrunk from 440,000 to just 260,000, with productivity well over 5 percent.[2]

Early in his career as CEO of GE, Welch acknowledged that the greatest improvement in productivity would come from the people, and the inspiration of each employee.

Welch, like all visionaries of elite companies, put his focus on closing management gaps. Despite outcry from traditionalists both inside and outside GE, Welch drove relentlessly to instill a constancy of purpose, a trusting culture, and the skills for instant adaptation in GE.

Acting in Zero Time: Rapid Adaptation

GE under Jack Welch has become the most competitive organization in the business world. It is as nimble as an entrepreneurial company yet has the might of a major corporation.

GE's nimbleness and adaptability are apparent in its changing business portfolio. Between 1981 and 1990, GE divested itself of many of its businesses, including traditional entities such as Central Air Conditioning and Housewares. In the process, it freed up $11 billion of capital. At the same time, the company aggressively moved into the new market opportunities by acquiring a whopping $21 billion worth of new businesses in the technology, financial services, and news media industries. GE has changed from a predominantly consumer goods manufacturing company to primarily a service company. Specifically, more than 85 percent of the GE profit in 1980 came from manufacturing, whereas today, more than 75 percent of profit comes from services. GE was able to achieve these rapid changes because of its investment in the development of a constancy of purpose and a trusting culture.

GE is reinventing itself once again by adapting
to the Internet Revolution.

As of this writing, GE is reinventing itself once again by adapting to the Internet revolution. For example, GE's Power System Division is aimed at becoming a "home aggregator" by offering customers the Internet-based Electricity Management Service, which helps customers to monitor their appliances.[3] NBC, a GE subsidiary, has multiple Internet assets, including its financial network, CNBC, which will integrate its television channels with its Web site to offer online financial products to NBC viewers. Rapid adaptation is becoming second nature to GE, despite its size.

New Perspective: Empower People

Early in his career as CEO of GE, Welch acknowledged that the greatest improvements in productivity would come from the people and the inspiration of the individual employees. In a 1990 interview, he described this belief: "I think that any company that's trying to play in the 1990s has got to find a way to engage the mind of every single employee . . . If you're not thinking all the time about making every person more valuable, you don't have a chance."[4] True to form, Welch increased the depth of his executive ranks. Many of GE's former executives, like Larry Bossidy, have become prominent CEOs of successful companies. GE has invested heavily in developing a broad and deep talent pool, a major factor in its success. Welch sums up his philosophy this way: "Getting great talent, giving them all the support in the world, and letting them run is the whole management philosophy of GE."[5]

Preparatory Action: Have Constancy of Purpose and Trusting Culture

When Welch stepped in as CEO of GE in 1981, he inherited a 100-year-old icon of corporate America with a record annual net income. Under the glossy image, however, GE was resting on its laurels, rotting away under the weight of its previous success, much as IBM and GM had done.

He saw globalization and boundarylessness as inevitable. He wasted no time in beginning the reinvention of GE, first by getting its bottom line under control to immediately consolidate and delayer the company's various functional businesses in order to increase agility. He then kicked off a 10-year initiative to change the minds of GEers. Welch bought preparatory time for GE.

Constancy of Purpose

Welch focused on tapping into the potential of each individual employee as the key to true competitiveness. He became a relentless force in the company, to create a shared vision, to educate each individual on GE's purpose, and to provide the fuel to ignite the people in his organization. Welch says, "Good leaders create a vision. They articulate the vision, passionately own the vision, and relentlessly drive it to completion."[6]

Purpose

To define GE's core purpose, Welch and 5,000 GE employees spent three years to reach consensus. The following statement of GE's belief system is the result of this massive effort.[7]
GE leaders, always with unyielding integrity:

- Create a clear, simple, reality-based customer-focused vision. They are able to communicate it straightforwardly to all constituencies.

- Set aggressive targets, recognize and reward progress, while understanding accountability and commitment.

- Have a passion for excellence, hate bureaucracy and all the nonsense that comes with it.

- Have the self-confidence to empower others, and behave in a boundaryless fashion. They believe in and are committed to workout (a 10-year initiative) as a means of empowerment; are open to ideas from anywhere.

- Have, or have the capacity to develop, global intelligence and global sensitivity. They are comfortable building diverse and global teams.

- Have enormous energy and the ability to energize and invigorate others; stimulate and relish change. They are not frightened or paralyzed by change; they see it as an opportunity, not a threat.

- Possess a mind-set that drives quality, cost, and speed for a competitive advantage.

To make sure that GEers actually live the stated GE values, an 80-page booklet titled "Integrity: The Spirit and the Letter of Our Commitment," was distributed to every employee in

1987.[8] Violators of this policy, once identified and proved as violators, are dismissed. The process is widely publicized in order to send a universal message of the importance of "living" the common values.

Furthermore, Welch and his managers evaluate people using a two-dimensional grid (see Figure 8.1) to identify four types of managers.[9] Type 1 delivers on commitments and shares the values; type 2 does not meet commitments nor share the company values; type 3 shares the values but does not deliver on commitments; and type 4 delivers on commitments but does not share the values of the company. While it is easy to identify and eliminate type 2 managers, Welch also encourages his people to weed out the type 4 managers, as he considers living the common values to be far more important than that of making commitments.

Given that GE has more than 260,000 employees worldwide, it is impossible to expect all of them to abide by the values all the time, despite the enormous effort made to motivate in the selection and training processes. Nevertheless, the number of such incidences has been statistically small as a result of Welch's constant push to ensure that all employees abide by the common values.

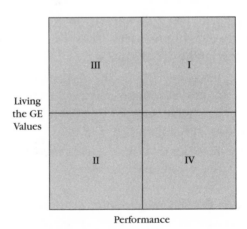

Figure 8.1 Jack Welch's four types of managers.

Compelling Vision

Perhaps Welch's most stunning accomplishment during his reign at GE has been the compelling vision he wove into the cultural fiber of the company. His message is clear: Every employee at GE was to focus on three concepts that would guide their actions no matter how many different markets GE entered:

- Become number one or two in every market GE serves.
- Integrate diversity.
- Erase boundaries.

The allure of working for a corporation with no boundaries and integrated diversity, combined with the basic desire to be number one (or number two) proved to be compelling enough to propel GE to success. Today, GE is the leader in 10 diverse markets, including industrial motors, medical systems, plastics, financial services, transport, power generation, information services, aircraft engines, electric distribution equipment, and television broadcasting. In addition, GE is second in the household appliance and lighting markets.

Welch created a mandate that all GE business units would rank first or second in their markets or be fixed, sold, or closed.

Clearly, the first part of Welch's message, become number one or two in every market GE serves, paved the way for GE's top ranking in so many markets. Welch supported that message with the concept of integrated diversity, whereby the different business units shared people, technology, financial data, and best practices, while maintaining their independence. The integration provided the necessary critical mass and conglomeration of resources to implement aggressive programs aimed at market dominance, while the diversity allowed GE to pursue a wide variety of markets.

Similarly, the GE concept of operating without boundaries brought each business unit into closer contact and collaboration with both customers and suppliers, yielding rich feedback and profitable partnerships. The destruction of both internal and external boundaries encouraged an openness to new ideas that led to the innovations in marketing, sales, product development, and, ultimately, top rankings in 10 markets. Welch is fond of telling the success stories of boundarylessness: "We quickly begin to learn from each other: productivity solutions from Lighting; 'quick response' asset management from Appliances; transaction effectiveness from GE Capital; cost-reduction techniques from Aircraft Engines; and global account management from Plastics."[10]

"I want a company where every single job grows
to the size of its owner's spirit."

—J. Welch

As a result of Welch's steady guidance and his three key goals, GE has changed significantly since Welch stepped in as CEO in 1981. The company has been transformed from a primarily domestic company to a global powerhouse, shedding many of its old businesses while boldly entering new business areas such as news and e-commerce. Specifically, between 1981 and 1990, GE sold off more than 200 businesses but it acquired more than 370 new businesses, including Kidder Peabody and Employers Reinsurance in financial business; NBC television (through its acquisition of RCA); and Thomson/CGR in medical equipment.

As GE continues to grow, and as its markets continue to unfold and expand, GE maintains its steady course, its constancy of purpose, under the guidance of this three-pronged approach. But Welch, knowing that no company survives, much less flourishes, on concepts alone, also devised action-oriented strategies for instant adaptation to support GE's continued growth.

Trusting Culture

As Welch streamlined the corporate hierarchy, he handed more power to the people in the business units, setting a few over-arching goals and trusting his employees to find the solutions. "If we are to get the reflexes and speed we need, we've got to simplify and delegate more—simply, trust more."[11] For example, after he set the goal that GE would be number one or two in every market it served, he trusted his business unit leaders and their staffs to find their way to success.

However, at the time, the GE corporate culture lacked the trust it needed to make such sweeping delegation of responsibility an immediate success. The GE culture was more like a country club, inwardly focused on playing the game and following orders.[12] Therefore, to cultivate a trusting culture, in 1988, Welch kicked off an ambitious 10-year initiative called workout. Workout started with four major objectives:

1. *To build trust.* To enable GE workers, regardless of rank or title, to speak candidly.

2. *To empower employees.* To tap into people's knowledge, as people closest to a given task usually understand both its inner workings and problems, and to tap into their emotional energy while giving them more responsibility.

3. *To eliminate wasteful work.* To achieve higher productivity.

4. *To establish a new paradigm for GE.* To involve the entire organization in the creation of a boundaryless organization.

At its inception, the workout program was designed to encourage people to speak candidly, so managers were locked out of these discussion sessions to preclude the possibility of retribution. At first, employees would meet in small groups of 30 to 100 for three days, and most spent the time venting complaints. Eventually, however, the sessions became more productive, as employees began actively solving corporate issues and problems.

In the second phase of the program, which started in 1990, workout sessions became more focused, with a clearly defined problem and a mandate to find a solution. In this phase, employees who normally worked together on cross-functional teams were brought together, and outside facilitators were no longer used to guide the sessions. The new focus and internal leadership of the program firmly grounded it as a core part of GE's culture and success.

Speed, simplicity, and self-confidence
are the cornerstones of success in
GE's organizational structure.

The Change Acceleration Program, which launched the third phase of the program in 1992, set a goal of training all GE managers as change agents, ensuring that the program could perpetuate itself forever. Today, a typical three-day workout session begins with a manager identifying some problems, then leaving. The participants break into small groups and tackle different aspects of the problem with the help of a group facilitator. At the end of the session, the manager returns, listens to the proposed recommendations, and makes immediate decisions. Some proposals are accepted, others are rejected, and still others are delayed for further investigation. Finally, as the last step of the session, a team is named and given a deadline to reach decisions on the delayed proposals.

The workout program is an unprecedented and wildly successful experiment in corporate America, both in terms of scale (GE has a goal of pushing all its people through the workout program) and scope (all processes are under investigation). The program has become a formal mechanism for sustaining continuous performance improvements and for transferring power to the workers. As a result of the workout program, GE has established a trusting culture that promotes direct communication between management and workers and that produces concrete measurable improvements in productivity and service.

Leadership Development

GE developed a comprehensive five-phase approach to leadership development: selection, development, stretching, evaluation, and reward.

Selection. Historically, GE, like most of its competitors, followed the traditional approach of hiring new employees on the basis of technical competence. Then, as Jack Welch began to empower his employees to participate in corporate decision-making processes, the selection criteria was broadened to include not only technical prowess but also the leadership skills of facilitation, problem solving, interpersonal abilities, and a willingness to share and teach others.

"Good leaders create a vision. They articulate the vision, passionately own the vision, and relentlessly drive it to completion."

—J. Welch

Development. To streamline management hierarchy and increase GE's agility, Welch shattered the sacred traditional institution of lifetime employment. Then he replaced it with the concept of lifetime *employability,* ensuring that GE's workers would continue to improve their career skills and be employable by any company over their working lifetime. For example, GE has spent more than $800 million a year on training and educational programs, including heavy investments in its Crotonville, New York, facility, GE's flagship training center, even during the company's massive downsizing efforts in the 1980s.

Stretching.   At GE, employees are constantly being stretched; that is, they are always expected to improve their performance, to work better, faster, using fewer resources all the time. For example, for each business unit, GE management will first estimate reasonable and achievable performance targets for profitability, cycle time, and other key measures. Subsequently, the goals are then set at a much higher level, encouraging employees to stretch their imaginations and skills to achieve these goals. Specifically, Welch created a mandate that all GE business units would rank first or second in their markets or be fixed, sold, or closed.

To maintain his employees' focus on stellar achievement, Welch constantly challenges them with the following five questions:

1. What does your global competitive environment look like?
2. In the past three years, what have your competitors done?
3. In the same period, what have you done to your competitors?
4. How might they attack you in the future?
5. What are your plans to leapfrog over them?

Welch's "stretching" strategy demonstrates his philosophy that no one ever knows the heights he or she can reach until challenged by a rigorous, ambitious goal. In fact, even failure to meet such a lofty goal usually reaps richer rewards than those earned by achieving a lesser goal. For instance, in 1991, GE set two goals for its 1995 performance: a 15 percent operating margin and 10 inventory turns.[13] Though the company failed to reach that goal, its performance was nonetheless astounding, with a 14.4 percent operating margin and almost seven inventory turns.

Evaluation. GE is one of the few companies truly driven by meritocracy, where promotions are awarded based on results. At GE, each person is evaluated by a diverse group that includes peers, subordinates, and supervisors. The evaluations not only measure financial performance and product or service quality, but include team-based measures such as demonstration of corporate values and beliefs. Indeed, the GE culture places greater importance on organizational management than on individual career management. To maintain the strength and integrity of the business units as individuals grow, move up the career ladder, or leave, Welch emphasizes the importance of developing succession plans for all key jobs.

To keep its top management at peak performance, Welch and three of his top executives travel annually to each of GE's 12 business units to review the company's top executives. These annual sessions, called C sessions, are "intensive reviews that force those running the unit to identify future leaders, make bets on early career 'stretch' assignments, develop succession plans for all key jobs, and decide which high-potential executives should be sent to Crotonville, New York, for leadership training."[14]

Reward. Welch believes reward is one the key motivating factors that inspire people to grow, stretch, and dedicate themselves to the corporate vision. Welch also recognizes that appropriate rewards, aligned with corporate values, are key to attracting the top talent in the industry to the company. Welch radically restructured GE's compensation plan, making recognition and compensation commensurate with risk and performance. Today, more than 27,000 people have stock options in the company, compared to the previous policy of granting options only to senior executives. In addition, bonuses and incentive pay are a significant part of the compensation package.

Rewards are highly individualized, with emphasis on total team achievement. For instance, although GE set a 4 percent salary increase as a companywide goal in 1998, some individuals were awarded pay increases of up to 25 percent without promotions; and bonuses reached as high as 70 percent of base pay for certain individuals.[15] Welch also seeks to offer spiritual rewards in addition to monetary ones: "I want a company where every single job grows to the size of its owner's spirit."[16]

Trust in People: Flexible Organizational Structure for Rapid Action

Recognizing that the market was filled with lean and hungry startups, which were inherently more agile than GE by nature of their size, Welch's first move as CEO was to delayer the management hierarchy, reducing the number of layers from 10 to 6. Welch says, "The way to harness the power of these people is not to protect them, not to sit on them, but to turn them loose, let them go, and get the management layers off their backs, the bureaucratic shackles off their feet, and the functional barriers out of their way."[17] The massive streamlining effort reduced the resistance and complexity of communication within the company, empowering it to respond more quickly to changing market conditions. For instance, prior to Welch's delayering efforts, the reporting structure

---

"If we are to get the reflexes and speed we need,
we've got to simplify and delegate more—
simply, trust more."

—J. Welch

---

for business units was lengthy and difficult; business unit leaders reported to senior vice presidents, who then reported to executive vice presidents. Today, business unit leaders report directly to the CEO's office, which includes Welch and his vice chairmen. This simplification of the reporting structure was but the first of Welch's campaign to break down barriers within the company.

Welch's next focus was on process simplification. Delayering the management hierarchy revealed numerous areas in which business processes were unnecessarily complex, the legacy of the prior management team's need for control and validation. Welch insisted that the organization embrace simplicity, knowing that it reduces resistance and accelerates the velocity of an organization. Simple designs reduce maintenance and reach the market faster; simple messages travel and are understood more quickly; and a simple compelling vision increases the speed of decision making within the company. Welch's message: Simplicity is the key.

As GE flattened and streamlined its organizational hierarchy and business processes, workers were transformed, too. The elimination of middle managers gave workers more authority in their work, and the new culture encouraged employees to interact with their supervisors as equals rather than as subordinates. Out of these cultural changes, GE workers gained a steady new self-confidence that, in turn, produced the ability to share, listen, take risks, and act decisively.

Speed, simplicity, and *self-confidence* are the cornerstones of success in GE's organizational structure. In cultivating these three qualities, Welch created a boundaryless organization, one that is fluid in structure and characterized by democracy, informality, and candor. Within this culture, people, ideas, and information move across functional and hierarchical lines with relative freedom. This internal freedom is then extended to include GE's family of suppliers and customers, so that when GE workers lack information or know-how, they do not hesitate to seek help from outside sources.

In today's digital age, where geographic boundaries are non-existent and the marketplace shifts minute to minute, GE's fluid organizational structure is clearly ready to adapt to new conditions in an instant.

Mutual Trust: Knowledge Sharing

Knowledge sharing and transfer are key to GE's success today. People in large corporations typically hide the areas in which they lack knowledge. Not at GE. Welch proclaims, "Today, with advanced information systems and a flat organizational structure, everyone has simultaneous access to the same information; everyone can be part of the game."[18] For example, a London manager in GE Capital shared his concept of using young people as mentors to teach their superiors about the Internet. "Within days, the order went out that every senior manager at GE, from Mr. Welch down, should spend a couple of hours a week being bossed around by an 'Internet mentor.'"[19]

"Today, with advanced information systems
and a flat organizational structure, everyone
can be part of the game. "

—J. Welch

When Welch came to power, one of GE's biggest weaknesses was the "not invented here" syndrome, whereby management and workers alike were reluctant to adopt ideas and innovations not internally generated. A costly legacy from founder Thomas Edison, who produced new ideas and products on a regular basis, this close-minded approach hindered GE's ability to adopt best practices from other companies.

Recognizing this weakness, Welch assigned Jack Frazier, of GE's business development unit, to find and study elite companies worthy of emulation. Frazier selected nine companies and, with his team, identified these key success strategies for GE to adopt:[20]

- *Process focus.* Use process maps to discover new opportunities for improvement, and manage process rather than people.
- *Continuous improvement.* Establish continuous innovation and improvement as corporate values, and instill them as part of the culture.
- *Customer satisfaction.* Use customer satisfaction as the primary measurement for performance evaluation.
- *Suppliers.* Consider suppliers as partners.

Based on Frazier's findings, Welch initiated a best practices course at GE's flagship training center in Crotonville, thus launching a "learning culture" within the company.

The GE learning culture is perhaps demonstrated most effectively by the Corporate Executive Council (CEC), a 30-member forum composed of GE's top leaders, business unit leaders, the vice chairmen, and Jack Welch. The CEC meets for three days each quarter to discuss not only the performance of the corporation and its business units, but also interesting new technologies and product development breakthroughs. These executives trade lessons learned as well as best practices.

For instance, when GE's medical systems business found success in using remote diagnostic technology to monitor its CT scanners in hospitals, so that the company could remotely detect and repair impending problems, often before the customer had even detected a problem, the technology was immediately shared with and implemented in other GE businesses, including jet engines, locomotives, and power systems. The shared technology resulted in increased customer satisfaction and lower cost structures for all the business units.

As a result of the best-practices initiative, many GE managers realized that they were measuring the wrong things. An example is given by the head of the corporate audit staff: "When I started 10 years ago, the first thing I did was count the $5,000 in the petty cash box. Today, we look at the $5 million in inventory on the floor, searching for process improvements that will bring it down."[21]

Sharing of knowledge has become a
cultural value that supports GE's
continued market dominance.

To solidify the learning culture, Welch aligned the corporate incentive system to reward those who shared their best practices freely over those who kept the best practices isolated. In short, the sharing of knowledge, whether at the executive or worker level, has become a cultural value that supports GE's continued market dominance.

Messages for Managers

The GE case highlights several important lessons about becoming an Instant Adaptation company:

- *In a hyper-growth, hyper-change economy, size is not a liability if it is guided by constancy of purpose and a trusting culture.* GE has all of the "liabilities" of a big, established company, but it has been able to put those aside, or better, turn them into assets in order to become more nimble and responsive. The leadership's constancy of purpose and the organization's trusting culture help GE flourish.

- *People are the key to the success of companies, but companies need to have the right kind of people and stretch them to accomplish more than they expect.* At GE, Welch is famous for helping people see beyond their perceived capabilities, which helps both the employee and the company.

- *Intellectual change leads physical change.* Change must occur first in people's minds before physical change can occur in the organization. GE effectively changes people's minds through its workout initiatives, which enable employees not only to learn about the goals of the organization, but also to try out new ideas to help keep GE in its leadership position.

- *Real change takes commitment.* GE is pushing every member of its 260,000-plus organization through the workout sessions. The cost of such an initiative, as well as its coordination and follow-up in implementing recommended solutions, takes a huge commitment on the part of the senior executives. But the benefit is also enormous, as illustrated by GE's performance.

- *Knowledge sharing is key to a trusting culture.* GE's success demonstrates that when the organization empowers its workers, and when trust is both infused and practiced by a company, amazing results can happen. "Bringing good things to life" is not only the slogan of GE; it reflects on the management practices GE has been using to keep its leadership position in every industry it enters.

Closing Process Gaps: Instant Execution

TO THRIVE IN THE AGE OF DIGITAL COMMERCE, ELITE COMPANIES are acquiring the very characteristics that make their technology so successful: speed, accuracy, and flexibility. In the area of business processes, these companies have designed their core processes to operate with the same fast speed and zero resistance of superconductors, which allow electrical pulses to pass through at maximum speed without interference from forces that cause resistance or drag. These companies exemplify the discipline of Instant Execution.

To illustrate this idea, consider Ford Motor Company's well-known accounts payable process redesign.[1] It's a classic example of reengineering a business process. The new process not only eliminated paper invoices from most vendors, but it streamlined the flow of information and, ultimately, reduced

Table 9.1   The Essence of the Zero Process Gaps Discipline

Current practice	Process improvement and automation
New perspective	No touch, no boundaries
Preparatory action	Agility
	Zero defects

the amount of time it took Ford to pay suppliers from weeks to, in some cases, hours. The process became instantly executable and the process was resistance-free for the majority of invoices.

Although this case is often discussed as an ideal example of reengineering, it is much more. It illustrates redesigning a process for zero resistance. Ford's new process executes instantly, releasing a check to a supplier when the goods are received on the dock, without any human intervention. It is an example of closing process gaps. The essence of the Instant Execution discipline is described in Table 9.1.

Current Practice Creates Process Gaps

Process gaps occur when the customer wants one thing but the process produces something else. The customer may want variety, but the process is inflexible. The customer may want instant information, but the process takes too long to deliver.

Process gaps occur when the customer wants one
thing but the process produces something else.

The customer may want to exchange physical transactions for virtual ones, such as sending electronic invoices but the process requires paper. Process may also stop at the boundaries of the organization, which do not allow documents to flow between the company and any outside organization. In short, gaps occur when there is a disconnect between what the customer wants and what the process delivers.

Gaps also occur when processes are poorly designed. Processes that have bottlenecks, nonvalue-added tasks, or long internal wait times between steps are poorly designed. Processes that require managerial approvals can cause gaps. Processes that produce poor-quality output cause gaps. These gaps force rework, which is costly and time-consuming. When people manually perform tasks that could be executed more efficiently by a computer, gaps appear in the process.

Finally, gaps occur when there is resistance in the process. Resistance can come from five sources (see Table 9.2). Often, individuals cause resistance when they do not have the correct knowledge or skills to do the work, or when they simply refuse to do the required work. Technology causes resistance because of faulty programming. Technology also causes resistance when it is unable to respond. How often have you

Table 9.2   Sources of Resistance

Source of Resistance	Example
Technological resistance	Work cannot be done because computer is down or network is not fast enough.
Process resistance	Work cannot be done because steps in process are complex, difficult, or not easy to complete.
Structural resistance	Work cannot be done because an approval is needed and the manager with authority is unavailable.
Organizational ambiguity	Work is not done properly because individuals do not understand the goal of the organization.
Cultural resistance	Work cannot be done because the culture rewards individuals with information, so no one wants to share.

been told your request could not be processed because the computers were down? That is technological resistance.

There are other, perhaps more subtle, forms of resistance. The process itself can cause resistance. Process resistance is the result of tasks that are inappropriate, overly complex, handled by too many people, or exceed the authority of those involved in the process. Some processes are just inappropriately designed, while others have come into existence as a natural result of daily work, without an overall design. This type of natural evolution leads to complex, stressful, and costly processes.

The essence of instant process execution is the philosophy "do the right thing, and do things right."

The structure of the organization can also block a process, as when managerial approvals are required in the process, or when the process reaches a boundary between departments, business units, or organizations. Often, just crossing the boundary is difficult because of the gaps to be traversed.

The culture of an organization can create resistance. For example, if the organization has a culture that rewards individuals who hoard information, then processes that require the sharing of information will face a difficult cultural block. Organizational ambiguity also causes resistance. Vague objectives and goals produce resistance in individuals who need clarity to meet organizational goals. Otherwise, they lack the guidance to take the next right step.

This discipline is about closing these gaps and removing resistance. But it's more than just automating an existing process, and it's more than just building a Web page as a portal to people-intensive internal processes. Automated processes that "pave the cow paths" often just speed up parts of the overall process. These cow paths, which represent the current processes, simply increase the speed of the wrong process, just as paving cow paths may result in paving the wrong "streets." Cow paths work for cows, not for cars; thus, paving them is not the way to build streets. Likewise, automating current processes just to speed them up is not effective for the Zero Time organization.

Using the Instant Execution discipline means seeing the process from a different perspective and optimizing the right set of activities. Consider the way traffic flows on the highway. If there is a traffic jam along the route, no matter how fast one can travel over certain sections of the route, the rate-limiting portion will still create a traffic jam. Adding more lanes to the freely flowing part of the route will not decrease the throughput time because it does not affect the bottleneck. In fact, it may worsen the situation by delivering more traffic, at a higher velocity, to the congested area. In contrast, examining the cause of the traffic jam and solving the root cause of the problem will improve the throughput time. Just as seeing differently allows the traffic engineer to redesign the highways, seeing differently allows managers to design processes for Instant Execution.

Acting in Zero Time: Instant Execution

The essence of instant process execution is the philosophy "do the right thing, and do things right." Instant Execution companies are careful to define processes clearly, keeping only those processes that are necessary, that add value. For Instant Execution companies, excess or inappropriate processes are excess baggage, which serves only to delay the delivery of instant customer gratification. Thus, Instant Execution companies put significant focus on defining clear and appropriate processes. This does not mean that they specify all of the steps of the process, but they do identify business objectives, the actions, and tasks needed to achieve those objectives, and the skills and knowledge needed to perform any manual tasks (see Chapter 5, Closing Learning Gaps: Instant Learning).

Instant Execution companies know that to close the gaps they must build instantly executable processes (see Figure 9.1). Instantly executable processes produce exactly what the customer wants because the process does not execute until the customer makes a request. This closes the gap between what the customer wants and what the process produces. Instantly executable processes ensure that the processes are designed appropriately, and include only value-added tasks. More important, instantly executable processes are designed for zero resistance.

Rather than improving or streamlining processes that have little or no impact on the effectiveness of the business, Instant Execution companies constantly scrutinize their processes from the standpoint of the customer. Processes that have a direct impact on the company's ability to serve its customers are considered critical and are designed for Instant Execution.

These companies design their critical process to require as few human "touches" as possible, and to cross organizational boundaries easily and without resistance. These processes, based upon sound, basic design principles, operate continuously

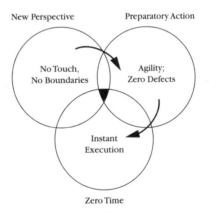

Figure 9.1 Essence of Instant Execution.

and automatically. Processes that are not continuous cannot execute instantly.

Design Processes for Continuous Operation

Because continuous operation is so critical to Instant Execution, in Instant Execution companies, the core business processes never stop. In part, these processes are able to run continuously because they have been designed with the "no-touch" standard, and hence do not require people. Processes continue to operate even when workers leave for the day. Moreover, processes in Instant Execution companies are designed to flow continuously, without queues or backed-up inboxes with unfinished paperwork. These companies understand that the customers in the digital age demand the ability to access processes 24 hours a day, 7 days a week, which makes continuous operation a requirement.

In the digital age, business never sleeps,
and companies seeking success will have
to create processes that operate continuously.

Continuous operation is not a new concept. Many companies have historically spent enormous resources staffing their organizations to operate round the clock. For example, manufacturing firms often operate with three shifts for continuous operation, as do help desks staffed with technical experts, or catalog companies that maintain a full staff to enter orders 24 hour a day. The difference between this kind of continuous operation and the continuous operation in Instant Execution companies is that within Instant Execution companies, continuous operation is combined with no-touch processes. That is, the number of people required to keep the processes running continuously is zero. This allows Instant

Execution companies to operate continuously without expending massive resources to staff operations day and night.

For instance, the University of Texas, like many organizations, has put most if its benefits process online, enabling consumers to access and update their benefits information at any time. When the annual benefits selection process is offered during the summer, employees can log in to the system and make their choices online. Those selections are recorded, and a confirmation is automatically sent to the employee. The process requires no clerical input to change or update the benefit information. Hence, the process offers significant options for customers by allowing them to access these services at any time, without the need for increased staff.

In an Instant Execution organization, processes
rarely require human intervention, so employees
are hardly involved in process execution.
Rather, people manage the exceptions.

Companies increasingly are using the Web to offer continuous access to their business-to-business customers. An article in the *New York Times* described an application created by Mobil Oil that enables more than 300 lubricant distributors to use an Internet ordering system to obtain products.[2] This has streamlined the process, and saves Mobil $100,000 a year in ordering costs; in addition, the error rate has been reduced from 30 percent to less than 1 percent. Business-to-business connections on the Internet are the latest incarnation of Electronic Data Interchange (EDI), and can be an initial step in building processes for continuous operation. In the digital age, business never sleeps, and companies seeking success will have to create processes that operate continuously.

New Perspective: No Touch, No Boundaries

To design an instantly executable process, managers of Instant Execution companies see differently. They boldly envision their processes to have the minimum number of touches and to be able to cross any necessary boundaries with ease (see Figure 9.2). In traditional companies, gaps occur because of handoffs between individuals, but Instant Execution companies can envision processes without gaps, in which all handoffs occur within the information system, resulting in systems that operate without delay. Gaps occur when a process is delayed because of organizational boundaries. For Instant Execution companies, however, even these handoffs occur seamlessly because the organizations on both sides of the boundaries have established links that make the process flow smoothly.

No touch means that Instant Execution companies design their processes to execute without human intervention. No touch goes far beyond the concept of automation. Automation is simply "paving the cow paths." In automation, a manual process is moved onto the computer, without any regard for

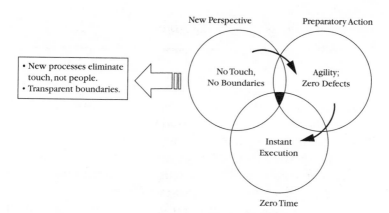

Figure 9.2 Instant Execution: new perspective.

handoffs, or intervention, by people. For example, a process that requires approvals from managers is a process that requires human intervention. As a result, although some parts of the process clearly move faster because of automation, the step that requires human intervention, the manager approval, limits the speed of the process and causes delay. Automation only incrementally increases the speed of the process; it is far from Instant Execution.

On the other hand, the Instant Execution companies, designing the same process to meet the no-touch standard, might create algorithms within the process for automatic approval, sending only exceptions or certain types of transactions for managers to approve offline. Likewise, a process that requires individuals to verify accuracy or match documents would, when automated, simply ship the documents electronically to the individual. In contrast, a no-touch version of this process would electronically verify accuracy or match documents, sending only the exceptions to the person. No-touch processes are automated processes that have been redesigned so that human intervention is not needed.

Automation only incrementally increases the speed of the process, but it is far from Instant Execution.

The eToys Web site demonstrates the benefits of a no-touch process implemented online. The Web site allows customers to search for specific toys, and alerts them when a choice is out of stock. If an item is out of stock, the system asks the customer if he or she wants to place a back order. The site also takes payment information, allowing customers to pay with a variety of credit cards. eToys then processes the order electronically and automatically sends the customer an e-mail confirmation the same day, telling the customer to expect a shipment within five to seven days. Faster shipping is offered for an additional fee. Once the customer has entered the appropriate information, the order entry process activates instantaneously. Back-order information, alternatives, and search capabilities allow the customer to complete the entire ordering process without human intervention from eToys. No eToy employees are required to handle the order until it is ready to be packed for shipping. Credit cards are electronically approved, inventory is electronically verified, and confirmation is instantly sent. This order entry process is a no-touch process that takes place entirely within the information system, allowing eToys to conduct business without a staff. The process flows without any resistance, which means that eToys generates revenue 24 hours a day, 7 days a week without needing to staff a sales force around the clock.

New Processes Eliminate Touch, Not People

While Instant Execution companies eliminate touch from the process, they do not eliminate people; even in this digital age, customers value human interaction. To meet that need, the Instant Execution company is strategic in deploying its staff. Consider retail banks and their use of cash machines, or ATMs.

ATMs are the portal of a no-touch process that allows customers to check their bank balance or withdraw cash without intervention by employees of the bank. If a problem occurs in the process, the bank is either located nearby or a phone is provided so the customer may seek a teller's assistance. Thus, the ATM process, like all no-touch processes, eliminates the majority of bottlenecks. Moreover, Instant Execution companies are

---

"The ideal organization lets people do what they
do well, and computers do what they do well,
and doesn't try to make one do the other's task."
—*Randy Fields*

---

careful to ensure that the elimination of bottlenecks does not make the process unsafe. In general, the 80/20 rule applies. That means Instant Execution companies remove the requirement for management approvals, employee verifications, and document matching for the 80 percent of the transactions that are routine; the remaining 20 percent, differentiated by size, exceptions, need for face-to-face contact, and other unique criteria, are handled by people. This strategy allows Instant Execution companies to deploy their employees to the greatest effect.

In an Instant Execution organization, processes rarely require human intervention, so employees are hardly involved in process execution. Rather, people manage the exceptions, constantly improve the processes, and interact with customers to provide a personal touch. People also build new systems, processes, and procedures; scout for new ideas; and coach other people. People are the faces associated with digital businesses. As Randy Fields, formerly of Mrs. Fields Cookies and more recently founder and CEO of the software development company Park City Group, is fond of saying, "People do some things very well, like interact with other people. Computers do some things very well, like perform repetitive processes. The ideal organization lets people do what they do and computers do what they do, and doesn't try to make one do the other's tasks." This division of labor, made possible by no-touch processes, is key to developing Instant Execution.

Transparent Boundaries

Instant Execution companies question everything when it comes to designing processes, and especially when examining the boundaries that exist both inside and outside the organization. They do not go to the extreme of eliminating all barriers, recognizing that some often are crucial to maintaining the security and integrity of corporate information; rather, these companies scrutinize the necessity of the barriers found at each boundary. Instant Execution companies reduce barriers to the minimum and create transparent boundaries wherever possible. One of the most famous examples of transparent boundaries is found at Proctor and Gamble, which shares product databases across a transparent boundary with Wal-Mart. It enables Proctor and Gamble to be immediately alerted when any Wal-Mart store needs product replenishment.

While the Instant Execution company eliminates touch from the process, they do not eliminate people, since in this digital age, customers often value human interaction.

As pioneers of e-business (business-to-business on the Web) and e-commerce (business-to-consumer on the Web), Instant Execution companies are keenly aware of the need to implement applications and "channels" that facilitate business and information flow across external corporate boundaries. While the network for e-business and e-commerce clearly exists, the software applications and organizational commitment that actually drive the flow of information between organizations must be designed for transparent boundaries. For example, in the mid-1980s, shoe manufacturer Nike, Inc. used the concept of transparent boundaries to build its interorganizational network. Its system linked designers in Oregon with contractors in Taiwan through Nike's CAD/CAM system, where prototypes were developed and tested. This enabled the company to seamlessly exchange information during each phase of the production process, from product design through manufacturing. Without such transparent boundaries, Nike would have experienced significant delays in the geographically widespread product development process.[3]

Transparent boundaries require a climate that allows for the sharing of information across boundaries. Many organizations create corporate value statements around teamwork and sharing, then continue to reward individuals who demonstrate their worth by "knowing more." These individuals are rewarded for hoarding information. In contrast, Instant Execution companies reward the individuals who share information and support teamwork. For instance, managers in Instant Execution companies set up cross-functional teams to facilitate discussions between departments, and they use e-mail, intranets, bulletin boards, and other technologies to encourage the sharing of information when face-to-face meetings are not possible.

Instant Execution companies reward the individuals who share information and support teamwork.

One technology that Instant Execution companies monitor closely is the security system, which more often blocks than facilitates the transfer of information across boundaries. While they are aware of the importance of safeguarding against theft and vandalism, Instant Execution companies choose technologies that both provide security and enable the transport of information across boundaries to selected suppliers, customers, and stakeholders. For example, virus detection software is a technology that offers security while also facilitating information exchange. The software scans files that seek to cross the barrier set up by the company, and allow only safe files to pass through, while stopping, correcting, and possibly eliminating infected files. The software actively prevents viruses from contaminating the system without interfering with the basic processes within the computer.

As a final step in creating transparent boundaries, Instant Execution companies give part of their core business processes to the customers and suppliers most affected by the process. For instance, as discussed in Chapter 4, Federal

---

Instant Execution companies give part of their
core business processes to the customers and
suppliers most affected by the process.

Express gives its high-volume customers a terminal from which
they access the company's database and track the status of
packages. Customers with lower shipment volume can access
the same information over the Internet, making the boundary
between Federal Express and its customers for shipping information utterly transparent. For Instant Execution companies,
no business process escapes intense scrutiny as they strive to
remove the barriers that erect unnecessary boundaries between themselves and their suppliers and customers.

Preparatory Action: Aim for Agility and Zero Defects

In order to create no-touch, no-boundary organizations, Instant
Execution companies develop the necessary core competencies of zero defects and agility. The goal of a well-designed process is Instant Execution, to produce output that completely
satisfies the customer. Having a process that executes instantly
but produces errors or output that does not match customer
needs is self-defeating. On the other hand, a zero defects process, which produces quality output that satisfies the customer
but that takes a long time to execute, is also of little value, as,
increasingly, customers are demanding instant gratification.
Hence, zero defects is a crucial competency for the Instant
Execution organization (see Figure 9.3).

Instant Execution companies must also develop the core
competency of agility, which is the ability to instantly reconfigure business processes to respond to changes in customer
needs or the business environment. They must also be able to
instantly build new processes when current processes cannot

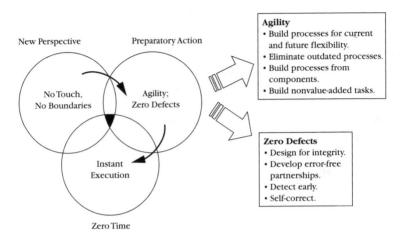

Figure 9.3 Instant Execution: preparatory action.

be adapted to fit new conditions. Agility and zero defects ensure the process speed, accuracy, and flexibility required to close process gaps to zero.

Agility

Agile processes are flexible, adaptable, and instantly configurable. Agile organizations invest in people and infrastructure to build robust, reconfigurable teams of people, equipment, and infrastructure. The agile organization makes effective use of technology and information to produce a high-quality product (see Figure 9.4). Proponents of agility describe it as a strategic, rather than tactical, method of challenging all paradigms of organization, management, production, and competitiveness.[4]

Further, though agility experts suggest that there is no formula for agility, there are guidelines that can help companies become more agile.[5] Those guidelines are summarized in Table 9.3. Agility is important to the Instant Execution discipline because the processes, and the organization supporting them, must be centered on customer-perceived value. Both

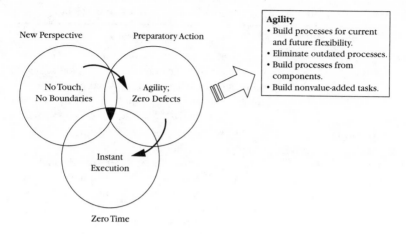

Figure 9.4 Preparatory action: agility.

agility and Instant Execution value the customer perspective, and build flexible organizations and processes around them. The concept of agility is an important foundation from which to implement Instant Execution.

The Instant Execution discipline also moves beyond agility. To create Instant Execution, organizations must be able to instantly create new processes so that old, unneeded processes can be removed as demanded by the business environment.

Instant Execution means processes
are *instantly* reconfigurable.

Having agility means that existing processes are reconfigurable; having Instant Execution means they are *instantly* reconfigurable. In addition, following the Instant Execution discipline means that new processes can be instantly built, while old processes can be instantly eliminated. Though we do not know (currently) of any organization that builds its

Table 9.3   Four Strategic Dimensions of Agile Competition

Dimension	Description
Enriching the customer	Perceived by customers as enriching them in a significant way. Products are perceived to be solutions to customer's individual problems, not generic solutions to those problems. Selling solutions, rather than products and services.
Cooperating to enhance competitiveness	Operational strategy of choice to bring products to market as rapidly and cost-effectively as possible. Cooperating through cross-functional teams, empowerment, reengineering, virtual companies, and partnerships in whichever configuration will leverage resources to provide what the customer wants. Values are built around short product-cycle times, intensity of relationships, and cooperation, to reach ultimate customer solution.
Organizing to master change and uncertainty	Thrives on change and uncertainty by building flexible organizational structures, which can rapidly reconfigure people and physical resources.
Leveraging the impact of people and information	Management nurtures an entrepreneurial company culture by distributing authority, providing resources, reinforcing mutual responsibility for joint success, and rewarding innovation.

Source: Inspired by S. Goldman, R. Nagel, and K. Preiss. 1995. *Agile Competitors and Virtual Organizations.* New York: Van Nostrand Reinhold Publishers, p. 5.

processes in this manner, it is the only way an organization can respond to customer demands instantly.

Build Processes for Current and Future Flexibility

Business processes must be flexible and adaptable in order to meet customer needs. Processes that support mass customization or small lot sizes often have this property. Flexible processes are those that can be easily adapted to changing customer preferences and that can produce exactly what the customer wants, even if it is slightly different from what any other customer wants. According to Kenneth Preiss in the *Agility and Global Competition Journal:*

> *In a lean system, the work processes between companies are linked together so as to optimize the production of a product. The product design process makes a serious effort to take into account customer opinions, but the end-user customer is not an interactive, intimate part of the design process. . . . An agile system, by definition, deals with incessant, rapidly changing demand and is distinguished by constant discovery of new customers and by including customer interactivity in the design of products in a long-term relationship.*[6]

For example, Nissan Automotive company's Kyushu assembly plant in Japan was built with flexibility in mind. High-technology production equipment was used to enable any model of any automobile currently in production to be made with any configuration. Each car on the assembly line can be completely different from the cars preceding or following it. The objective is very rapid assembly to customer order.[7]

Further, the Instant Execution organization is able to create new processes to respond instantly to customer demands. While the inputs and outputs of business processes may remain constant, the process itself must be able to be built instantly. For example, CNN, the television network owned by Turner Broadcasting, is often favorably cited for its handling of the Persian Gulf War. When war broke out, CNN instantly developed the capability to follow the events, building in whatever was needed to broadcast news instantly to its customers. The organization was built to create new processes as needed to provide service to its audience. CNN has a core competency in instantly creating new processes.

Eliminate Outdated Processes

Just as new processes must be automatically created, old processes must be automatically eliminated to keep the organization running efficiently. The Instant Execution organization is able to eliminate inefficient, ineffective processes as quickly and as easily as it is able to build new ones. Ineffective processes are a drag on the organization. They consume resources and often they get in the way of the work that must be done. Instant Execution companies are careful not to keep old processes for sentimental reasons. For instance, not only does CNN build new processes instantly to adapt to changing conditions, but when the news event that necessitated a new process is over, the company eliminates the unneeded process.

Just as new processes must be automatically created,
old processes must be automatically eliminated,
in order to keep the organization running efficiently.

Panasonic has built this capacity directly into its product cycles. At Panasonic, the consumer electronics product cycle time is three months, during which the next CD player, TV, VCR, or stereo component is designed, tested, and put into production. All the processes for a product overlap in order to meet the 90-day cycle. As soon as a new product comes into production, all processes related to the previous product are eliminated.[8]

Build Processes from Components

To be able to instantly create new processes and eliminate old processes, Instant Execution companies design their processes in a modular fashion. Process designers in these companies see each process as a set of components that can be linked in unending variations for instant reconfiguration.

Instant Execution companies build the modules and components of their business processes so that they can be assembled like Tinkertoys, connected and disconnected as needed to meet customer demands. Understanding how to identify and build components is a core competency of Instant Execution organizations.

For example, Hewlett-Packard's Web site, now offers extensive customer service online. Customers can access any component they desire in the online service process. Hewlett-Packard offers components that answer technical questions, take product orders, and download device driver software. Each of these services is a single component, updated individually as necessary, which saves the company from having to change the entire process with each update. By using these components, customers can virtually "build their own support process." Further, the company tracks how the site is used, a process that provides the company with reliable ideas for reconfiguration, updates, and new product enhancements. The site would be even more agile if it reconfigured itself, without human intervention, as the Knight Ridder Web sites do.

Knight Ridder, a publishing company that offers online newspapers among its many services, has created a set of extremely agile processes that support Instant Execution. As of the summer of 1999, Knight Ridder had more than 40 Internet news sites that provided services similar to those of the local newspapers. However, unlike the local newspapers, which must work through the arduous process of producing newspapers in physical form, these online news sites are designed to be automatically updated based on news stories collected by local newspapers. The Web sites are able to create new processes, as needed, to incorporate new stories. The software is able to identify key headlines as they are being written for the local newspapers and to format the articles for the

Web. This software also verifies that the headlines are not already posted on a site, to avoid duplication of work. Classified advertising is also done automatically. As an individual ad is sold, it triggers a process that automatically formats, indexes, and delivers the ad to the site. These Internet-based tools are examples of how organizations like Knight Ridder are building processes that instantly respond to the demands of their marketplace.

Eliminate Nonvalue-Added Tasks

Instant Execution companies use process redesign methodologies and principles to eliminate nonvalue-added tasks. They go back to basics when it comes to designing processes, and examine the fundamental way the processes should execute instantly. Table 9.4 lists Instant Execution design principles,

Table 9.4   Instant Execution Process Design Principles

- Organize around outcomes, not tasks.
- Don't pave the cow paths; redesign the process for instant execution.
- Have those who use the output of the process perform the process, to eliminate handoffs.
- Subsume information gathering and entering work into the real work that initially produces the information.
- Treat geographically dispersed resources as though they were centralized.
- Link parallel activities, instead of integrating their results.
- Put decision points where the work is performed, rather than sending work to a manager for a decision.
- Build controls into the process to insure integrity of outcomes.
- Provide customers with a single point of contact, and support that contact with information links to all relevant company information.
- Use information systems to handle routine tasks; use people to handle nonroutine tasks, and blend them together.
- Evaluate boundaries to remove barriers of information flow.
- Capture information once and at the source.

Source: Inspired by Hammer. July 1992. "Don't Automate, Obliterate." *Harvard Business Review.*

adapted from Michael Hammer, acknowledged as the father of reengineering.[9]

Once the process has been designed, Instant Execution companies constantly evaluate every step in their core business processes for value. They never stop asking questions that help identify nonvalue-added tasks. They evaluate the value added to the end customer by asking if the customer would be willing to pay for it. They evaluate value added to the company by asking if the company should pay for it. They evaluate each task to see if it is critical to the successful completion of the process.

If a task lacks value, Instant Execution companies do not hesitate to eliminate it from the process—instantly—by changing upstream tasks, automating tasks, or simply removing the task. Typical candidates for elimination are tasks such as checks, verifications, and corrections (see the next section on Zero Defects). Most of these tasks are performed manually and can be easily automated.

For CIGNA, a leading insurance and financial services firm, the basic process design principles yield rich results. In a recent process redesign project, CIGNA saved $2 to $3 for every $1 invested in redesign. Further, the company was able to reduce operating expenses by 42 percent, cycle time by 100 percent, while increasing customer satisfaction by 50 percent.[10] Based on a solid foundation of sound process design principles, Instant Execution companies create sound core business processes that are agile and flexible.

Set Zero Defects as a Goal

Most processes are designed with inherent flaws, which results in defective output. In most organizations, the solution is to inspect the output for defects, then rework them. For Instant Execution companies, which measure themselves against the zero defects standard, no defect is acceptable. Thus, rather than adding tasks for inspection and rework into their processes, they integrate tasks to identify and fix problems *before* they reach the end of the process. For example, consider the production line at Toyota Automotive Group that is built with the zero defects mentality. Workers have the authority to stop the line at any time to correct defects instantly, rather than waiting for errors to be found at inspection stations. The process encourages workers to allow only perfect systems to pass through the process. Instant Execution companies examine their processes for integrity, establish error-free partnerships, build in systems for the early detection of problems, and design processes for self-correction (see Figure 9.5).

Design for Integrity

Instant Execution companies carefully design and analyze their processes and process components to ensure integrity, which means they are deliberately designed to produce no defects. For example, one of the authors taught a computer science course using the "clean room" method, in which students were not allowed to compile their code until they were sure their program was bug-free. Although compilation is a necessary step to transform higher-level computer programs

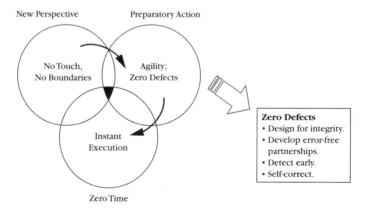

Figure 9.5 Preparatory action: zero defects.

into a language understood by the computer, students regularly used it to debug their code, since the compiler readily identified the location and nature of errors, or bugs. But this method of programming and debugging lacks integrity, since its focus is on catching errors *after* they have already been introduced, rather than on designing error-free programs. Students in the class were rewarded for writing code that compiled correctly the first time. One student later was employed by the Internal Revenue Service, and eventually wrote a program with about 20,000 lines of code that compiled correctly the first time. That program has been in use for more than 10 years and continues to run error-free.

Develop Error-Free Partnerships

To achieve zero defects, an organization must be able to ensure that the information and raw material inputs into the processes are error-free. Instant Execution companies often implement a certification process to identify the suppliers that guarantee error-free inputs. As is usual for companies practicing the Zero Time disciplines, Instant Execution companies view their suppliers as partners in the process rather than as adversaries (see, for example, Chapter 11, Closing Inclusion Gaps: Instant Involvement).

For example, Xerox reduced its suppliers from hundreds to fewer than 50 to develop these strategic error-free partnerships. Xerox orders large quantities of product from these select suppliers. In return, Xerox requires these strategic partners to guarantee that their product will always meet the company's quality standards, so that Xerox can send these products directly to the manufacturing floor without testing. As a result, Xerox was able to eliminate its internal testing group and significantly reduce cycle time.

External facing processes, which cross organizational boundaries, are not the only ones that need to be error-free. Internal processes, which pass information or products to other departments within the organization, must also produce zero defects. For Instant Execution companies, which create internal partnerships between departments, error-free strategic partnerships are key to developing zero defects, and every process is matched and measured against this standard.

Detect Early

While the goal of zero defects it to remove all sources of defects in order to produce error-free products and services, in practice, errors do occur. Thus, Instant Execution companies design their processes to include early detection systems so that errors can be corrected virtually before they occur, and certainly before the completion of the process. One method these companies use to detect errors before they become problems is regular maintenance of the machines and equipment that perform the processes. Instant Execution processes carefully watch for signals that indicate possible problems or failures.

For example, Otis Elevator Company installed a Remote Electronic Monitoring (REM) in its current line of elevators. The REM feature is a chip with detection and communications capabilities. If an elevator is about to fail, the REM feature detects it and calls an Otis maintenance and repair group at the field service office. A repair person is dispatched to the elevator to fix the problem, often before the building supervisor is aware that the problem exists. George David, former CEO of Otis Elevators, complained that the only time people noticed an elevator was when it was not working properly, causing only negative attention. To alleviate this problem, David built numerous systems to ensure his elevators not only ran continuously, but had early detection systems.[11]

Self-Correct

As a final step in creating processes with zero defects, Instant Execution companies develop self-correction features within their processes. The implementation of self-correcting processes requires process designers, during the design phase, to analyze all possible failures and ways to automate the correction process. In the Otis Elevator example, the service person is dispatched with the right tools and parts to fix the system often before the building supervisor detects the problem. In this way, the elevator system is both self-detecting and self-correcting because customers are never involved in the process. Otis takes care of it for them.

The essence of the Instant Execution discipline is building a zero resistance organization. Instant Execution companies see processes differently, develop the core competencies of zero defects and agility, and build processes that instantly execute.

Close Process Gaps

Operating in horizontal time means that there are gaps in business processes. The Instant Execution organization knows all about potential gaps in its processes, including handoffs, delays, nonvalue-added tasks, impenetrable barriers, inflexible processes, rework, and resistance. In Zero Time, process gaps are eliminated by designing processes for Instant Execution. That means seeing processes differently. Processes are designed with no touch and no boundaries. To meet this no-touch, no-boundaries standard, processes must be designed for agility and zero defects. Zero Time organizations have processes that are agile, have zero defects, and are well designed. The following are some basic guiding rules for the Instant Execution organization.

The processes of a Zero Time organization
must be flexible, able to be instantly created
or destroyed in order to stay in synchronicity
with the external environment.

A superconductor allows energy to flow without producing heat, since it encounters no resistance. The processes of an Instant Execution company must be superconductive. These processes are characterized by the following attributes:

- *No touch.* Processes are automated and require no human intervention.

- *No stops.* Processes are continuous, always accessible, and free from wait time or queues.

- *No waste.* Processes consist of only value-added steps.

- *No boundaries.* Processes are not constrained by artificial boundaries between departments, groups, or companies.

- *No defects.* Processes produce high-quality reliable products or services that meet customer specifications.

Unlike superconductors, the processes of an Instant Execution organization must be flexible and able to be instantly created or destroyed in order to stay synchronized with the external environment. Therefore, the components of an Instant Execution organization must be designed to be *recyclable.* Instant CUSTOMERization occurs with dynamically reconfigurable processes.

CHAPTER

Progressive Insurance: An Instant Execution Company

PROGRESSIVE INSURANCE IS ONE OF THE LARGEST INSURANCE companies in the United States. It works with more than 30,000 independent agents who sell the majority of Progressive's policies to all types of automobile drivers. At Progressive, more than 16,000 employees serve about 2 million policyholders. Founded in Cleveland, Ohio, in early 1937 by two lawyers, the company began by writing nonstandard

The authors would like to thank Willy Graves, president of Progressive County Mutual, and Texas state manager, for his contribution to this case.

195

Table 10.1   Progressive Net Premiums from 1988 to 1998

Year	Net Premium Written (in Billions)
1988	$1.2750
1989	1.1603
1990	1.1963
1991	1.3246
1992	1.4512
1993	1.8192
1994	2.4572
1995	2.9128
1996	3.4417
1997	4.6651
1998	5.2997

auto insurance. In 1965, Peter Lewis, the son of one of the founders, acquired a controlling interest in Progressive Casualty with the goal of becoming a full-service automotive insurance provider. The company went public in 1971, and by 1987 it had written $1.116 billion in premiums.

Since then, the company has experienced explosive growth. Table 10.1 summarizes the growth in net premiums over the past 10 years. The average annual rate of compounded growth over the past five years has been 24 percent, with net income increasing 11 percent. A shareholder who purchased 100 shares of Progressive for $1,800 at the initial public stock offering in 1971 would own 7,689 shares as of January 1, 1999, with a market value of $1,302,000. This reflects a 26.8 percent compounded annual return, which greatly outdistances the 9.5 percent returns achieved in the S&P 500 for the same period.

The company communicates a clear vision and set of core values. Following is Progressive's annual report vision statement:

We seek to be an excellent, innovative, growth and en-during business by cost-effectively and profitably re-ducing the human trauma and economic costs of auto accidents and other mishaps, and by building a recog-nized, trusted, admired, business-generating brand. We seek to earn a superior rate on equity and to pro-vide a positive environment, which attracts quality people who develop and achieve ambitious growth plans.[1]

Progressive Insurance prides itself on being an innovator in its field. The letter to shareholders in the 1998 annual report highlights this:

We offer auto insurance to every licensed driver, sell-ing many ways while innovating in claims, technol-ogy, pricing, and consumer brand building. We first changed the claim service so we could respond to most claims within a few hours of their being reported, any time, any day. Next, we made all services available 24 hours a day, 7 days a week, and developed rates for all licensed owners and drivers. Then we distributed in the many different ways consumers wanted to buy—in person from Independent Agents, by telephone through 1-800-AUTO PRO or online at progressive.com. Another innovation was offering competitor premium compar-isons. We use a combination of television, direct mail, and other media to urge consumers to consider Pro-gressive's unique combination of price and service. As important as Independent Agents continue to be to Progressive, we no longer depend solely on them choos-ing us for their nonstandard risks.[2]

As an innovator, Progressive delivers service very differ-ently from the competition. Managers have built a process that exemplifies Instant Execution: the Immediate Response initiative.

Acting in Zero Time: Instant Execution

Progressive's Immediate Response® initiative is an example of Zero Time thinking. The process was redesigned from the ground up, not just incrementally improved, to increase throughput and decrease cycle time.

Progressive's Immediate Response initiative is an example of Zero Time thinking.

The Immediate Response process begins when a customer calls Progressive to report an accident. The call center takes down preliminary information, such as the basic facts of the accident, and sets up the claim in the computer. If the claimant is still at the scene of the accident, a claims representative is sent in a company Immediate Response vehicle to begin the investigation and settlement. If the claimant is calling from home or some place other than the scene of the accident, then the agent taking the phone call transfers the call to a local branch where a claims representative gathers additional information. In either case, Progressive strives to resolve all coverage and liability issues as quickly as possible so that the claims representative is able to cut a check to the claimant during this initial meeting. Willy Graves, president of Progressive County Mutual, and Texas state manager, commented, "In about 20 percent of the first Immediate Response visits, we cut a check immediately."

Responding instantly to claims gives Progressive some important benefits. First, it gives claims reps immediate information about an accident. Graves explains: "We talk to the claimant while the accident is fresh on their mind. Sometimes people forget the details if you wait too long to talk with them." Second, the process allows Progressive to settle claims in minutes, instead of months or days. That gives claimants the money necessary to reconstruct their lives immediately after an accident, and it reduces the cost of settling claims. Third, instantly responding highlights to customers and potential customers the sense of urgency and the importance Progressive places on claims. Making sure the process happens instantly is important to CEO Peter Lewis. He describes the key advantages:[3]

- *Speed saves money.* Claims reps perform their inspections right after an accident, instead of waiting several days to visit customers. Eliminating delays generates cost savings. Vehicles that get inspected sooner get repaired sooner, which means Progressive pays fewer storage-lot and rental-car fees. And by enabling reps to focus on the real work of inspecting accidents, rather than sitting at a desk doing paperwork, Progressive hires fewer reps than it would otherwise need.

- *Speed helps customer morale.* The sooner a Progressive rep meets with an injured party, the more likely that party is to negotiate a settlement. "You're already mad because someone hit you," says Lewis. "If your insurance company moves slowly, you get furious. You're probably going to run out and get a lawyer. Then the process could take months or years and cost everyone more money."

- *Speed improves accuracy.* Claims reps who see vehicles immediately can assess the damage firsthand, which means that Progressive is less likely to be victimized by claims of inflated damage. "As much as 30 percent of the money that auto insurers pay out is for overpayment related to some degree of fraud," says Graves.

- *Speed lowers prices.* If a company spends less money settling claims, it can charge lower prices for its premiums. That's a huge benefit for a company that has built its business around insuring risky drivers, who are charged more for coverage. The faster Progressive has become, argues Lewis, the more price-competitive it has become.

- *Speed sells.* The company's track record of fast, on-site service has become its best marketing tool. The distinctive Immediate Response vehicles turn heads, whether they're roving the freeway like a billboard on wheels or parked alongside a wreck for every rubbernecker to see. "In some ways, responding to the scene is our best form of advertising," says Lewis.

By treating accidents as emergencies
rather than just as claims, Progressive saw
a new market opportunity.

The process executes instantly. When a customer calls, an agent immediately responds. Combining information technology with customer service has allowed Progressive to keep the "high-touch" feel, while using its information systems to record the case and networks to immediately locate and assign a claims representative. Combining all of these factors results in instantly executable processes.

New Perspective: The Claims Process

Progressive Insurance saw the white space other insurance companies did not see. By treating accidents as emergencies rather than just as claims, Progressive saw a new market opportunity. Graves explains:

We did some research on why consumers are so un-happy with car insurance companies. We found that one big reason was that insurance companies treated people who were in an accident like adversaries. At the point that a customer is involved in an accident, any accident, it is an emergency and should be treated as such even if there are no personal injuries. The typical claims process was designed to be convenient for the insurance company, not the claimant. Claims were handled so the workload of the claims department was predictable. We decided to change our perspective and treat claims as the emergencies they are.

In 1990, Progressive began offering its now-famous Immediate Response claims service. Progressive has customer representatives available 24 hours a day, 7 days a week, to process calls from customers involved in an accident. Often the call is answered at the corporate office, and a claims adjuster is dispatched. He or she arrives at the scene of an accident with a laptop, ready to process a claim, make on-the-spot decisions, and write the customer a check for repairs. In most cases, the company conducts its inspection within hours of when the accident is reported.

Progressive does not hesitate to cross boundaries or to share information with all. It embraces a concept called *information transparency,* a policy of sharing with customers information about prices, costs, and service. Reps will quote their own rates as well as rates of competitors, even if competitors' are lower. This is done to better inform customers of their choices, because Progressive believes better informed customers are better customers.

By being innovative and aggressive, Progressive Insurance can move quickly within its market. Combine that with seeing differently and Progressive consistently jumps way ahead of the competition. Seeing differently gives Progressive great benefits, including lower costs and greater customer loyalty. It also gives customers great benefits; primarily, they get their claims resolved quickly.

Preparatory Action: Design for Zero Defects and Building Agile Processes

At Progressive, taking preparatory action means building the components of the processes claim reps will need when the customer calls. With a strong focus on business processes, the company was one of the early adopters of the reengineering concept, as discussed in Hammer and Champy's *Reengineering the Corporation.*[4] For example, business leaders are also process leaders, who drive both a line of business and a business process. In the fall of 1999, there were process leaders for claims, products, direct marketing, agent marketing, and Internet marketing. Process leaders report to the CEO and sit on the policy team, along with the head human resources officer, the chief information officer, the chief financial officer, and the chief investment officer. According to Graves, who also served as the leader of the claims process from 1996 to 1998, "Our core processes have to do with marketing, product development, and claims. The actual processes we do change with the dynamics of the market, but the leaders of those processes are some of the highest officers in the company."[5]

"We help our customers when and where they need it most, at the actual accident scene."

—*Values cited on Progressive's Web site*

But Progressive has also designed processes that minimize defects. In the insurance business, zero defects means no operational errors by the insurance companies or claims errors by fraudulent claims. By this measure, Progressive's Immediate Response claims process has eliminated many defects other companies still experience. Errors occur because the damage to be repaired may not have been a result of the accident, or because claimants report problems that are not entirely accurate. Operational errors occur because of hand-offs within the company in the process of handling claims. Errors are typically corrected by "rework," which results in some claims being processed over and over until resolution is secured.

At Progressive, the new process eliminates the need for much of this rework by reducing or eliminating these types of errors. Since claims adjusters visit the accident site, they are able to take pictures of the damage before anything else happens to the car. Likewise, they can investigate the accident while it is still fresh in everyone's mind, reducing the likelihood of loss of critical details.

In addition to focusing on zero defects, Progressive designs its processes for agility, to respond to every aspect of the customer's needs. For Progressive, this means handling calls on a wide range of issues. Some customers are calling from the accident site, and in those cases Progressive can dispatch an agent directly to the site. Others are calling from home, and their calls are handled by an in-house agent, who may come see the car at the home or may have the claimant visit a claims center for an evaluation, depending on the condition of the vehicle. Some callers are at the body shop, in which case Progressive will work directly with the body shop to resolve the claim. The process is extremely flexible and is instantly reconfigured to meet whatever the customer needs.

Progressive exemplifies the Zero Time concept of preparatory action. The company has designed its processes so it can respond easily and immediately to the multiple situations that clients present. Progressive has negotiated contracts with body shops, has formed relationships with car-rental agencies, and has thoroughly analyzed and improved all aspects of the claims process *before* it is actually needed by customers. This careful effort, in advance of actual need, is an excellent example of preparatory action.

How Does Progressive Do It?

Progressive offers round-the-clock service because its customers want access to claims adjusters when it's convenient for them. This means building a culture and an infrastructure that can respond to support this level of service. The culture is built around five core values, as summarized in Table 10.2.[6]

Every employee action at Progressive is directly influenced by these values. From CEO Peter Lewis to Progressive's newest employee, each person is aware of these values and strives to incorporate them into all business activities. These

Table 10.2   Progressive's Five Core Values

Core Value	Description
Integrity	We revere honesty. We adhere to high ethical standards, report promptly and completely, encourage disclosing bad news, and welcome disagreement.
Golden rule	We respect all people, value the differences among them, and deal with them in the way we want to be dealt with. This requires us to know ourselves and to try to understand others.
Objectives	We strive to communicate clearly Progressive's ambitious objectives and our people's personal and team objectives. We evaluate performance against all these objectives.
Excellence	We strive constantly to improve in order to meet and exceed the highest expectations of our customers, shareholders, and people. We teach and encourage our people to improve performance and to reduce the costs of what they do for customers. We base their rewards on results and promotion on ability.
Profit	The opportunity to earn a profit is how the competitive free-enterprise system motivates investment to enhance human health and happiness. Expanding profits reflect our customer's and claimants' increasingly positive view of Progressive. We value all people's well-being and strive to give back to our communities.

Source: Progressive's 1998 Annual Report, p. 7.

values are an integral part of the annual reports, and are included on the corporate Web pages. In fact, these values are spelled out on the corporate Web page titled, "What makes Progressive progressive?" which includes the philosophies that have driven Progressive's rapid growth:[7]

- *Caring . . . both on and off the roads.* Our vision is to reduce the human trauma and economic costs associated with automobile accidents. We do this by providing our policyholders with services designed to help them get their lives back in order again as quickly as possible.
- *Immediate Response claims service.* At the heart of our success is our Immediate Response service, our ultra-fast, 24-hour claims service. We help our customers when and where they need it most, at the actual accident scene.
- *Living by the golden rule.* Progressive continues to succeed by following the golden rule—a "core value" of Progressive, stressing respect of others, valuing their differences, and finding ways to serve them. We're committed to becoming the auto insurer of all people, offering a range of competitively priced auto insurance options so that everyone can live part of the American dream by safely "taking to the road."
- *Simplifying the process.* We make it easy for people to choose the policy that's right for them through our free auto insurance rate comparison and shopping service. In just minutes, you can get an insurance quote from Progressive (as well as comparison rates of three other market leaders) by calling 1–800-AUTO PRO or visiting our Web site at progressive.com. We're the only U.S. auto insurer to offer this kind of "apples to apples" rate comparison with our competitors. If satisfied with the Progressive quote, you can purchase a policy in any of three easy ways: online, over the phone thorough the 800 number, or with one of our 30,000 independent agents located throughout the country.

- *Customer service to beat the band.* Our customer service representatives are available any time of the day or night to answer questions about policies, payments, and account status. Computer-savvy customers can access information online by visiting our award-winning Web site.

A team of seven to eight people carries out the process. A typical team has three representatives in the field, each of whom visits accident scenes and body shops or goes wherever the automobile is. Three work as inside representatives, answering the phone and managing the claims through the process. Usually, another person works as a dispatcher, sending assignments to the field representatives; and an administrative support person, assists the team with administrative details. In some cases, a separate team leader functions as a quasi-supervisor. This person is responsible for quality assurance, and does on-the-job training, which might involve riding around with a field representative or sitting at the desk of an inside representative.

From CEO Peter Lewis to Progressive's newest employee, each person is aware of the values and strives to incorporate them into all business activities.

The Instant Response claims process is designed to be "quick and seamless, with an unbroken flow of information between the customer, Progressive's central database, and the local claims operation."[8] The claims representative, who works on the phone to help customers with claims, will submit a task assignment, which results in a dispatched field adjuster visiting the customer's home. He or she also radios or pages the corresponding claim number so the field adjuster can download the customer's file into his or her laptop. This handoff insures that field adjusters have immediate access to all information about the claim they are working on.

The Claims Workbench is a software application that helps field reps do transactions more easily. Three key tools make information immediately accessible to all team members. First, field representatives can get their assignments electronically through their diary. The diary contains the date, time, and tasks to do. It records all their appointments, including those made for them by the rest of the team. The dispatcher typically enters an assignment in the rep's diary and the rep downloads it to his or her laptop while in the field. The second tool allows the field rep to enter new status notes into a file. *Face sheets,* the forms used to record notes about a case, are electronically accessed on the laptop and downloaded to the company mainframe when the laptop is connected to the network. That keeps the case files current throughout the company. The third tool lets the field rep retrieve all other notes and face sheets on the case entered by others on the team. In that way, every team member has access to all the information about a file. The former head of Progressive's claims information technology department, Mark Smith, believes this application gives Progressive a major strategic advantage.[9] It moves information instantly from wherever it is to wherever it needs to be, so that claims adjusters can do their job instantly.

Combining information technology and people has allowed Progressive to keep the "high touch" feel. [They use] their information systems to record the case and [use] networks to immediately locate and assign a claims representative.

The infrastructure also supports the Immediate Response claims service. Progressive's 1998 annual report stated:

Our customers come to depend on this level of service, which we support by continuous real-time monitoring of internal systems performance, threatening weather, and other natural disasters. This approach allows us immediately to reconfigure voice and data networks and to activate disaster response teams when required.[10]

What Will Progressive Do Next?

Making sure customers get their reimbursement quickly has been the focus of the Immediate Response claims service. But customers may need more in the aftermath of the accident. Graves gives an example:

In one case, our representative saw a claimant within a few hours of an accident. He handled the case as we had hoped, talking to claimants, looking at the cars, taking pictures of the accident, and giving the owner of the car an initial check. That is the way it is supposed to happen. But then the next entry in the computer was 10 days later. And then 70 days later, when I reviewed the file, not all aspects were completely resolved. It turned out that we did the initial response beautifully, but we lacked following up appropriately. Closure is the wrong measure, because the case is not closed when the initial check is cut. We looked at "last payment" and found it took significantly more time than "instantly." So we are building in metrics and incentives to insure that the follow-up happens and to make sure the whole resolution is completed as fast as possible.

In keeping with the goal of making it easy for customers to get through the after-accident tasks, Progressive has begun partnering with automotive body repair shops. It aligns with body shops that have the same goal: satisfying customers fast. And it is signing them up as partners in delivering service to customers. As of fall 1999, more than 400 shops were in the

Progressive network, and those shops covered virtually all geographical areas of Progressive's business. When successful, Progressive will have extended its Zero Time processes across boundaries to the shops that repair autos for customers, thereby streamlining the next act in the postaccident scenario of customers.

Progressive will have extended their Zero Time processes across boundaries to shops who repair autos for customers, streamlining the next headache in the post accident scenario of customers.

Another initiative, called Autograph, which uses global positioning system technology, is being test-marketed in Texas. The customer gets a quote from Progressive with a minimum and maximum price for insurance, and a tracking device is installed in the car. The device tracks how much and where the customer drives, and the rate is adjusted accordingly. The tracking device can also be used as a security device, which helps Progressive with claims. During early tests of this service, the device was installed in a car that was subsequently stolen from a shopping center parking lot. The device recognized that the thief was not an authorized driver, and the system called the police. The car was automatically shut off, and the thief ran away; the tracking device guided police to the car, which was returned to the parking lot, almost before the customer knew what had happened. This system will allow Progressive to expand its services even further.

Messages for Managers

Progressive strives to be an Instant Execution Organization with innovative new approaches, including instant settlement. Here are the lessons we can take from the case:

- *Build instantly executable processes by focusing on exceeding customer expectations.* This is about thinking differently as to how business can be done fast, not about how to speed up the existing processes. It is based on a vision of instant execution.

- *Provide instant executable processes, which benefit both the customer and the company.* Building instantly executable processes provides quick response to customers; it also reduces the number of resources needed. Progressive's Immediate Response claims service closes claims more quickly, saving Progressive the time it takes to review and revisit most cases. Cutting the check instantly saves Progressive from building that activity into a settlement department. Statistics from the company show that its claims costs decreased relative to its competition with the implementation of this initiative.

- *Automating existing processes will not bridge the process gaps.* If Progressive had just speeded up its claims resolution process, things might have happened a bit faster. But by rethinking the entire process, and challenging itself to deliver service instantly, the company was able to leapfrog even the best automated claims resolution system in the business, and now it leads the industry and has set the benchmark to beat.

- *Identify and redesign processes that touch the customer.* Progressive implemented the Immediate Response claims service, then went further to partner with body shops to make the claims process even easier for customers. Customers who choose Progressive now have their accident claims resolved more quickly, and can get their car fixed with minimum hassle, all under the Progressive umbrella.

Closing Inclusion Gaps: Instant Involvement

SUCCEEDING IN THE AGE OF DIGITAL INFORMATION ISN'T ABOUT being the Lone Ranger; it's more about being one of the Magnificent Seven. Just as companies can no longer afford to rely on a single visionary leader to guide them to success, Instant Involvement companies know that they must gather a band of complementary and supporting forces—in the shape of suppliers, customers, and complementary partners—to create an ecosystem to battle competitors and win market dominance.

Many elite companies, sensing the need for partnership and collaboration with both suppliers and customers, have invested heavily in Electronic Data Interchange (EDI) whereby companies link up with customers and suppliers via computer, to exchange invoices, payments, and inventory information. For instance, Wal-Mart, commonly cited as a leading company in EDI, has developed such a tight connection with suppliers that anytime the company's inventory drops below a safety level, orders are automatically generated and sent to suppliers. Wal-Mart also shares information on competitor sales, markdowns as a percentage of sales, sell-through versus current inventory, and numerous other detailed measures. Wal-Mart and its suppliers have both captured huge cost and cycle time savings as a result of EDI.

Clearly there are benefits from electronic supply chain management systems, but even these are not enough to close the gaps.

Nevertheless, despite reaping the many rich rewards of EDI, elite companies like Wal-Mart have no time for self-congratulations. They know that EDI is but the first stepping stone to the true partnership and collaboration with suppliers and customers that breed longevity in the marketplace. For Zero Time companies, nothing less than Instant Involvement will suffice. The essence of the Instant Involvement discipline is described in Table 11.1.

Instant Involvement means that anyone who can improve the company's supply chain is automatically and instantly involved in doing so. Instant Involvement is all about the

Table 11.1 The Essence of the Instant Involvement Discipline

Current practice	Supply chain management
New perspective	Tightly coupled ecosystem
Preparatory action	Mutual commitment
	Strategic partnership

inclusion of every relevant, necessary person or company in the corporate supply chain processes. It is about building an ecosystem for the business. This does not mean that Zero Time companies involve every person in every decision. Rather, they collaborate so closely with their partners, across organizational and process lines that employees from partnering organizations automatically consider themselves part of the Zero Time company's efforts to improve supply chain performance.

Instant involvement means that anyone who can improve the company's supply chain is automatically and instantly involved in doing so.

Current Practice Creates Inclusion Gaps

Gaps occur in the supply chain when a supplier is not ready to deliver the needed parts or services. For example, when a customer wants to place an order, most organizations react. If inventory levels are too low, they order parts from their preferred vendors. If they have an electronic supply chain, they electronically send the request to their suppliers. But gaps still occur. Suppliers are not always able to respond quickly enough. Suppliers may not be organized in a way to respond to the requests. That produces a gap in the supply chain.

Gaps occur when parts arrive, but not in the quantity needed or at the quality level required. Suppliers have their own processes, which may not match with the company's. In the absence of strong relationships and in the presence of a simple buyer/supplier relationship, it is assumed that the buyer not the supplier, will inspect, test, and reject parts that are not up to speed. Although enlightened suppliers take on some of these tasks, it is not enough. Companies need to be able to count on their suppliers every time, all the time. Gaps occur when they cannot, when a company cannot deliver customer demands because the supply chain is not instantly responsive. Just building an electronic supply chain, where inventory information is electronically shipped to vendors does not solve the problem because it does not close the gaps.

The current organizational response to supply chain issues varies from the most simplistic systems to highly sophisticated networks of shared information. With the most basic supply chain management systems, when a customer order is placed, the supply chain is immediately alerted and parts are automatically ordered through the supply chain linkages with vendors. More sophisticated supply chain management systems extend the linkages with vendors by exchanging forecasting and inventory management data. With this extension, suppliers can check and adjust inventory levels automatically, and shift production schedules according to forecasted demand. In the age of Just-in-Time (JIT) inventory delivery, such electronic linkages are critical. Traditional systems simply cannot shuffle paper fast enough to keep the process moving. Clearly, there are benefits from electronic supply chain management systems, but even these are not enough to close the gaps.

For Instant Involvement companies, the benefits resulting from the most sophisticated supply chain management system are insufficient because they do not bridge all the gaps. Nothing less than complete partnership with customers and suppliers will suffice. Unlike traditional supply chain strategies, which focus on improving operations within a company, Instant Involvement companies coordinate supply chain activities across company boundaries, *throughout* the entire chain.

The discipline of Instant Involvement addresses these problems. Where traditional companies seek electronic linkages with vendors, Instant Involvement companies seek intimate, long-term, trusting relationships with strategic partners. Where traditional companies focus on managing a single supply chain, Instant Involvement companies build an entire symbiotic ecosystem of mutual commitment around each chain. Or, as described by Chris Mann, the CIO of Visteon, Ford Motor Company's $18 billion parts division, "The conventional supply chain is no longer appropriate. It's not sequential. It's more like a web."[1] Instant Involvement companies have embraced this idea, developing the capability to integrate not only their supply chains, but the rest of their business as well. Michael Dell captures the essence of this idea: "If you don't create an integrated value chain, don't expect to survive."[2]

Acting in Zero Time: Instant Involvement

The key to closing these gaps is to instantly involve all members of the supply and value chains of the business. The minute the customer asks for something, the appropriate information is instantly fed to everyone in the supply chain who will be involved in responding to that customer. This level of dependencies requires companies to build solid partnerships with all parties involved. As such, Instant Involvement companies move beyond just establishing electronic linkages between their information systems and their partners'. They build an ecosystem based on mutual commitment and strategic partnerships (see Figure 11.1).

As with every other aspect of their business, Instant Involvement companies do not allow themselves the luxury of delay when involving their partners in business decisions. To improve their products and services, Instant Involvement companies involve not only customers and suppliers, but also complementors, organizations that do not directly interact with the company, but offer complementary products and services. The three groups are described in Table 11.2.

Whether involvement means bringing in suppliers to help make decisions about product development, linking with key vendors to share daily demand data so parts can be delivered just in time, or collaborating with customers to create high-value services, Instant Involvement companies develop the

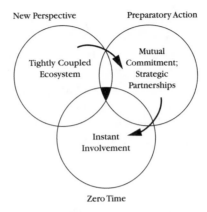

Figure 11.1 Essence of Instant Involvement.

linkages across organizations that guarantee speed of inter-action. For example, General Motors insists that its suppliers use a standard document interchange language to ensure a direct connection to GM's engineering and manufacturing processes.

Because developing these linkages can be expensive, Instant Involvement companies are careful in selecting their partners. Instant Involvement companies know their own

Table 11.2   Type of Groups for Instant Involvement

Type of Group	Description	Example
Suppliers	Firms that provide materials and services to the company.	Proctor and Gamble is a supplier to Wal-Mart.
Customers	Firms that use products and services produced by the company.	Car dealers are customers of General Motors.
Complementors	Firms that provide products or services used in conjunction with those produced by the company.	Intel and Microsoft are complementors.

capabilities thoroughly, so they know what kinds of partnerships they need, and, therefore, which companies to partner with. Instant Involvement companies also strengthen the connection to their partner companies by creating multiple linkages, as well as by creating an environment of free information exchange.

An Instant Involvement company's core competency
is its ability to develop and manage relationships.

Know Your Capabilities to Pick the Right Partners

"Know thyself" is key in choosing the right partners. For Instant Involvement companies, self-knowledge is the prerequisite that reveals the gaps in organizational capability. It is these gaps that Instant Involvement companies so effectively fill with perfectly coordinated partnerships.

For example, Benetton S.p.A., the well-known producer of knitted garments, is hailed for its success in building a solid business in the volatile high-fashion industry. For Benetton, the key to success is the self-knowledge that it excels in marketing and product design. Benetton, recognizing both its core competencies and its limitations, designs all clothes in-house, then outsources much of its production to strategically situated mills and manufacturers. Similarly, the company taps into its own marketing strength to create a strong demand for its products, but relies on logistics specialists to deliver the finished clothes to franchised retail stores.[3]

In examining its core competencies, Benetton has kept in-house the processes it does well, marketing and clothing design. All other areas are outsourced to contractors or franchisees. This precise understanding of strengths and weaknesses has guided this successful clothing retailer to find the perfect partners to fill the gaps and to provide a seamless, professional, fashionable image to the marketplace.

Link Supply Chains with Partners

While Instant Involvement companies are patient in cultivating long-term relationships with customers and suppliers, they become radically impatient with gaps in the supply chain. These companies strive for a completely seamless supply chain, wherein orders are placed, processed, and delivered with maximum ease and minimum human interference. Instant Involvement companies link supply chains with both customers and suppliers to conduct as much business as possible electronically, and hence automatically.

The ecosystem is so closely linked that members
actually keep each other alive.

For example, when the Hertz Corporation places an order with Ford Motor Company for fleet cars, Ford's supply chain management system not only launches the appropriate processes within the company, but also simultaneously alerts the suppliers of windshields, radios, tires, and steel of the impending order to ensure the Just-in-Time delivery of materials.

Industry pundits call this flurry of instant activity "value chain integration." Safeway, a growing supermarket chain in England, has taken advantage of the rapidly expanding World Wide Web to develop its integrated value chain online. On the buying side, hundreds of suppliers access the supermarket's data warehouse daily for real-time updates on product sales in each store in the chain, so that appropriate inventory adjustments can be made. This real-time access ensures that the supermarkets never run out of stock, while enabling suppliers to shift production schedules according to demand. Customers, of course, benefit from the wide varieties of products always in stock in every store.

On the selling side, the supermarket links up with customers online, providing remote shopping and electronic catalog services, as well as personalized promotions based on customer data gathered in stores and online. For customers seeking the convenience of online transactions, this electronic access translates into greater perceived value of the supermarket chain. Simply by linking its supply chain with both suppliers and customers via the relatively inexpensive World Wide Web, the supermarket has experienced a terrific growth in business.[4] More important, the integrated supply chain has provided value to all the customers in the supply chain, the ultimate goal of Instant Involvement companies.

New Perspective: Tightly Coupled Ecosystem

Instant Involvement companies envision an ecosystem, whereas their competitors see only supply chain management. Because Instant Involvement companies know that survival is one of the strongest motivators for success, they deliberately create a symbiotic relationship among the companies, suppliers, partners, and complementors that all depend on each other to succeed in the marketplace (see Figure 11.2).

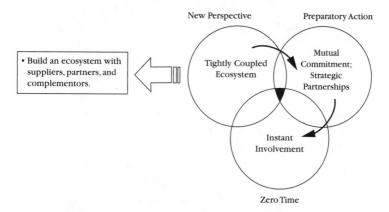

Figure 11.2 Instant Involvement: new perspective.

The members of the ecosystem are so closely linked that they actually keep each other alive. For instance, BOC Gas demonstrates the effectiveness of including both suppliers and customers in its ecosystem.[5] BOC Gas is a global distributor of industrial gases, with American headquarters in Murray Hill, New Jersey. A typical transaction within the BOC ecosystem proceeds as follows. BOC places a multimillion dollar order for tungsten hexaflouride, a highly toxic gas used in producing semiconductors, with its Japanese supplier located 7,000 miles away. Within minutes of receiving the order, the Japanese supplier not only has begun processing the order, but has notified the BOC distribution center in San Diego, California, that the order is on its way.

While such an ecosystem implies mutual benefits and mutual risks, each member remains independent, to encourage creative and innovative growth.

The entire exchange takes place over the World Wide Web, eliminating the need for multilingual phone calls, faxes, written purchase orders, invoices, or shipping notices. BOC purchases about $20 million worth of product from Japanese suppliers annually. The information about the product, which is negotiated and purchased in bulk once a year, is posted on a restricted-access Web site that is accessible only to select BOC suppliers, customers, and employees. As the order progresses through delivery, both suppliers and BOC update the status on the Internet, noting shipping dates, quantity, and shipping method. Customers are also invited to order products and check shipments online. The entire BOC ecosystem tightly links the success of BOC, its suppliers, and its customers through BOC's online transaction system, empowering BOC to influence and control the process. If one member of this system were to falter, the entire supply chain would be greatly affected.

While such an ecosystem implies mutual benefits and mutual risks, each member remains independent, to encourage creative and innovative growth. For instance, Intel is famous for sharing its product road maps not only with customers, but also with original equipment manufacturers and independent hardware and software vendors. This has led to a healthy ecosystem in which each participating company is able to take advantage of its knowledge of upcoming Intel products, while also understanding its role in supporting Intel's success.

Intel, in turn, taps the ecosystem members to gather product and inventory information, as well as ideas and innovations for future generations of microprocessors. As a result of this perfect coordination, Intel's ultimate customers receive magnified value, as the ecosystem produces not just improved microprocessor chips, but also a vast array of complementary products. The Intel ecosystem enables the company to leverage the resources of all the participating companies, not just those it can muster internally. In this way, Intel extends its reach, and becomes, in essence, an enormous virtual company that encompasses all its partners within the ecosystem.[6]

In the rapidly changing Instant Involvement company, the ecosystem functions as a source of stability. The strong relationships of participating members provide a solid base from which the Instant Involvement company can operate. The Instant Involvement company is freed from many traditional supplier problems; it does not have to continuously seek out

---

In the rapidly changing environment of the instant involvement company, the ecosystem is a source of stability.

---

new suppliers, which gives it more time to focus on value-added aspects of the business.

Preparatory Action: Make Mutual Commitments and Form Strategic Partnerships

In order to create a harmonious ecosystem, Instant Involvement companies use negative time to establish strong relationships with key partners, customers, and complementors. These relationships are based on mutual commitment, and more than just information is exchanged between the firms. The mutual commitment links not only the Instant Involvement company's survival with that of its partners, but also its growth and success. Within the relationship, partners complement each other naturally. An Instant Involvement company's core competency is its ability to develop and manage these relationships (see Figure 11.3).

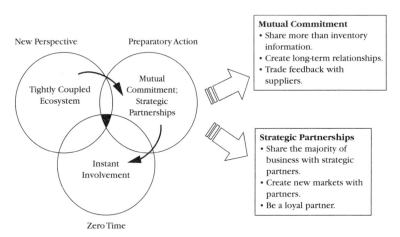

Figure 11.3 Instant Involvement: preparatory action.

Mutual Commitment

Instant Involvement companies recognize that for instant involvement to truly take place, each member of the ecosystem must demonstrate the same level of trust and commitment. Mutual commitment means giving each other access to critical, proprietary, and strategic information. For instance, at BOC Gas, the company grants its suppliers unprecedented access to its own inventory data to ensure that stockpiles are replenished. At the other end of the process, BOC customers, like Massachusetts Institute of Technology, invite BOC to enter data directly into its cost accounting system to avoid the hassle of double data entry as the order moves through the system. For both, trust in a partner company's commitment to mutual success is the core competency (see Figure 11.4).

Share More Than Inventory Information

Instant Involvement companies, having already implemented EDI, have a long history of sharing inventory information

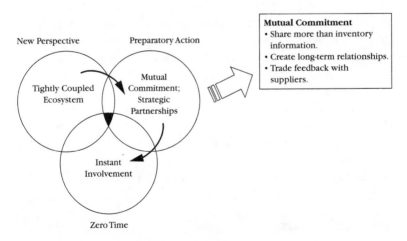

Figure 11.4 Preparatory action: mutual commitment.

with their suppliers. But they know that providing data to suppliers regarding what customers are ordering is just the beginning. An Instant Involvement company wants its suppliers to understand the needs of its customers intimately, and hence is constantly providing detailed customer data. These elite companies understand the perils of withholding data and forcing their suppliers to rely on guesswork to provide the appropriate products and services. Rather, because Instant Involvement companies have been careful to select top suppliers and to nurture an environment of trust, they are eager to provide the essential information that helps suppliers help them. They build a core competency around sharing all types of information.

Instant Involvement companies recognize that for instant involvement to truly take place, each member of the ecosystem must demonstrate the same level of trust and commitment.

Wal-Mart, a pioneer in supply chain management, uses a proprietary system called Retail Link to assist its suppliers. Originally developed to provide suppliers with easy access to sales, inventory, and shipping information about its own products sold in Wal-Mart and Sam's Club stores, Wal-Mart has expanded the system to share data over the Internet and provide more avenues for collaboration with suppliers. Through the system, suppliers now have access to two years' of sales history, plus the previous day's sales information for every one of the 2,400 Wal-Mart and 450 Sam's Club stores, by 4:00 A.M. the following day. Says Randy Mott, CIO of Wal-Mart, this system enables suppliers to "treat each store as if it were the only one in the chain."[7] Wal-Mart's open-door policy of readily sharing information with suppliers yields the considerable reward of customized treatment of each store by every supplier.

While Wal-Mart's work in supply chain management is well known, a lesser known company pet supplier PETsMART, has been blazing its own trails in this area.[8] Though it has a lower profile than Wal-Mart, PETsMART is not a small company, boasting 463 stores in North America, 95 stores in the United Kingdom (as of summer 1999), and annual sales of $2.1 billion for the fiscal year ending January 1999.[9] The company has linked its supply chain of global vendors via collaborative group over an extranet, to create an opportunity to work together on shared business objectives and processes. The primary application involves Lotus Notes and Domino software, and is used for merchandising workflow and retail business processes.

Beyond simply linking suppliers via the extranet, PETsMART offers a variety of forms and electronic processes to educate suppliers in designing products and packaging for speedy manufacturing and delivering. Overall savings from this intimate collaboration with vendors have accrued largely from reduced sample and mold creation, less travel, electronic quality assurance, computer-aided engineering, and shortened design time and time-to-market.

Both Wal-Mart and PETsMART, masters of the Instant Involvement principle, have flung open their doors to suppliers, to share more than just inventory information. Both companies have created far deeper partnerships, which guarantee supplier benefit and, hence, supplier loyalty.

Create Long-Term Relationships

Instant Involvement companies take a long view when it comes to forming relationships with vendors; they recognize that the cost of developing a new relationship is much higher than the cost of strengthening an existing one, thus they build a core competency in developing and nurturing these

Instant Involvement companies take the long view
when it comes to forming relationships with
vendors; they recognize that the cost of developing
a new relationship is much higher than the cost
of strengthening an existing one.

relationships. For companies like Wal-Mart, that often means helping suppliers upgrade their systems to Wal-Mart's standard of technology, as described in this extract from the company Web page:[10]

EDI has proven to be the most efficient way of conducting business with our product vendors. This system of exchanging information, purchase orders, invoices, etc. allows us to improve customer service, lower expenses, and increase productivity. Wal-Mart expects its merchandise suppliers to be able to participate in EDI transactions once they become Wal-Mart vendors and are assigned a specific vendor number. EDI packages range in price from minimal expense to highly sophisticated systems.

If you become a Wal-Mart vendor and do not currently have EDI capability, Wal-Mart will work with you to determine the EDI package that best meets your business needs, and that also meets Wal-Mart's EDI requirements. If you already have an EDI system in place when you become a Wal-Mart vendor, Wal-Mart will perform tracking tests to make sure your current system is compatible with Wal-Mart EDI.

Wal-Mart is an example of a company that consistently demonstrates its willingness and ability to be a good citizen, not only within the towns and cities where its outlets are located, but also with their vendors and suppliers. In addition to reducing the costs of interacting with suppliers, Wal-Mart managers are freed from having to establish these relation-ships over and over again. All relationships take time and investment, and Instant Involvement companies see value in establishing long-term relationships.

Trade Feedback with Suppliers

Instant Involvement companies, because they are just as committed to their supplier partners' success as to their own, are not hesitant to share feedback with suppliers. If suppliers, even certified supply partners, have difficulty delivering products and services that meet the stringent quality standards so commonly set by Instant Involvement companies, they are sure to hear about it. Because Instant Involvement companies see partnerships as a long-term proposition, they inform suppliers of unsatisfactory service, then help vendors find constructive solutions that benefit both parties. A core competency of mutual respect is developed.

Like everything within the symbiotic ecosystem, Instant Involvement companies expect the avenues of feedback to be two-way streets. Because of the intimate relationships developed over long periods of time, suppliers are familiar with many of the Instant Involvement company's systems, including purchasing, invoicing, manufacturing, and even information systems. As such, Instant Involvement companies regularly solicit their vendors for feedback, ceaselessly searching for the next quantum improvement that yields success.

Form Strategic Partnerships

For Instant Involvement companies and their partners, creating strategic partnerships means work, dedication, and commitment. Forming strategic relationships means more than just recategorizing certain vendors as "strategic partners." It means choosing wisely those vendors that demonstrate compatibility with the company's values, cultures, and beliefs. Further, it means selecting those vendors with the right level

It means choosing wisely those vendors that
demonstrate compatibility with the company's
values, cultures, and beliefs.

of quality, commitment, and willingness to go beyond the traditional customer/supplier linkages. It means developing a core competency in forming and cultivating these partnerships (see Figure 11.5).

Because Instant Involvement companies are so selective about choosing partners, they tend to develop an entire portfolio of vendors and form different relationships with each type. M. Bensaou, in the *Sloan Management Review,* describes four categories of suppliers: captive buyers, market exchange, captive suppliers, and strategic partners.[11] Table 11.3 summarizes the characteristics of each.

Consider General Electric's (GE) supplier base. GE's Trading Process Network is a Web-based link to its suppliers that enables them to make bids for GE component contracts. It features an electronic catalog, the ability to make electronic purchases, and the option to pay online with an electronic credit

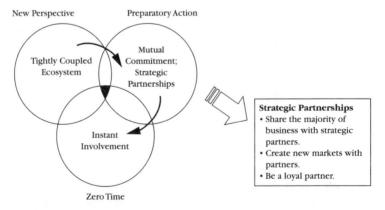

Figure 11.5 Preparatory action: strategic partnerships.

Table 11.3   Portfolio of Supplier Relationships

Buyer's Specific Investment	Supplier's Specific Investment	
	Low	High
High	**Captive Buyer**	**Strategic Partner**
	Customer makes high level of investment in people, time, effort learning about supplier, exchanging information and nurturing the relationship relative to the supplier in order to keep the supplier.	Both buyer and supplier have invested a high level of assets, resources, and effort to sustain the relationship.
Low	**Market Exchange**	**Captive Supplier**
	Neither buyer nor supplier has invested much in specialized assets to work with each other. Shifting to another partner is a low-cost proposition.	The supplier makes a high level of investment in the relationship in order to win the business from the buyer.

Source: Inspired by M. Bensaou. Summer 1999. "Portfolios of Buyer-Supplier Relationships." Sloan Management Review.

card. Its implementation is required of all GE suppliers. The system handles more than $1 billion worth of GE business annually. Yet despite the extreme convenience of the system, GE's supplier base has shrunk, because not all suppliers wanted or were able to make the shift to e-commerce.

In short, Instant Involvement companies find the strongest strategic partners in those companies willing to stake a significant aspect of their future on the partnership. Instant Involvement companies, having worked diligently to acquire

---

The sharing of business becomes the currency of trust between the company and its partners.

---

such valued partners, cherish and nurture these relationships, offering their partners lifetime value, a bulk of the business, and deep loyalty, even in times of trouble.

Share the Majority of Business with Strategic Partners

This is not to say that any company wants to be locked so tightly into relationships that it has no alternatives, but Instant Involvement companies cannot be afraid of commitment. To keep the supply chain running smoothly, the same values sought from customers downstream—lifetime loyalty and customer share—must be offered to suppliers upstream. Instant Involvement companies do not expect their strategic partners to shoulder the heavy burden of loyalty, which often requires the supplier to replace entire information systems or completely revamp business processes, without returning the favor.

As a result, Instant Involvement companies deliberately share the bulk of their business with those vendors that are willing to commit their loyalties. This sharing of business becomes the currency of trust between the company and its partners. It is the incentive that encourages partners to continuously place the welfare of the partnership high on the list of priorities. For example, Cisco Systems, the manufacturer of routers and other parts needed to build and run the Internet, is well known for its supplier relationships (see Chapter 12 for the Cisco case study). Cisco gives the bulk of its business to its strategic partners, like Solectron. The ties with Solectron enable Cisco to give them the bulk of its orders for printed circuit board assemblies with confidence.

Create New Markets with Partners

Beyond improving the product or service quality through strategic partnering, Instant Involvement companies also find that such partnerships yield access to new and different markets. Though their partners are part of the same ecosystem,

they often work in significantly different markets, thus bringing insight on how Instant Involvement companies might
expand or grow. In fact, it is often the case that strategic partners will develop a breakthrough innovation but lack the
funds or resources to introduce it to the marketplace. In such
cases, partners look to the Instant Involvement company to
share risk and joint-venture the product, often creating new
markets for both companies.

Instant Involvement companies see an ecosystem,
whereas their competitors see only
supply chain management.

For instance, South African fruit conglomerate Capespan
found that partnering with IBM created a new marketplace
through which to sell its products. Thanks to IBM's innovative
technology, Capespan is able to reach retailers throughout the
world, which had previously been out of reach for the regional
company. With IBM's technology, the company plans to allow
global retailers to order electronically from Capespan *and* all
of its partner growers and suppliers. Capespan will funnel
order information to its partners to improve production planning and predictability of suppliers. Capespan is also working
with partner IBM on least-cost distribution projects, wider
product ranges, and industrywide initiatives in electronic commerce to improve its business opportunities.[12]

Be a Loyal Partner

For Instant Involvement companies, being a loyal partner is a
value that is built into the formula for strategic partnering.
This value means that Instant Involvement companies are
loyal especially when their partners are in trouble, jumping
in to assist in whatever ways possible. In essence, taking on
strategic partners results in increased switching costs for

Instant Involvement companies. It is very much like taking on a marriage partner. Because Instant Involvement companies invest so much in first scrutinizing, next selecting, then developing their partnerships, switching partners midstream becomes an extremely costly endeavor. More important, switching harms the company's reputation and ability to get a new high-caliber partner.

Instant Involvement companies rarely conceal
information from their partners, knowing that
if they have selected their partners wisely,
sharing of information can only help.

In order to prepare for instant involvement, Instant Involvement companies build the core competencies needed to form the necessary partnerships for instant involvement.

Close the Inclusion Gaps

Instant Involvement companies are adept at identifying key strategic partners and at bringing them in as members of an extended family for the purpose of mutual collaboration and benefit. Because the effort involved in nurturing such relationships can be labor-intensive, not to mention very expensive, Instant Involvement companies choose partners wisely, then carefully create the optimum conditions for success. Instant Involvement companies maximize the following critical success factors:

- *Choose the right partners.* Instant Involvement companies are highly selective in choosing partners, limiting themselves to those that are perfectly compatible with the company's vision, values, and methods of conducting business. Instant Involvement companies do not view every vendor as a partner; they select only the best-performing vendor in each strategic area.

- *Link electronically with partners.* Instant Involvement companies tie their partners into their corporate intranet, with the goal of sharing electronic information instantaneously. Instant Involvement companies make every effort to ensure that partners meet their high technological standards, acknowledging that making careful IT investments in partner companies will eventually reap rewards for both parties.

- *Eliminate surprises.* Instant Involvement companies openly communicate and share information with partners, constantly seeking ways to help or share risks with partner companies. Instant Involvement companies rarely conceal information from their partners, knowing that if they have selected their partners wisely, the sharing of information can only help, not hinder. Instant Involvement companies develop the corporate value of information sharing, both internally and within their partner companies, and make that value an obvious part of their culture.

- *Focus on long-term relationships.* Instant Involvement companies are patient; they know that it takes time to establish the trust and confidence that comprise the currency of solid, mutually beneficial partnerships. Instant Involvement companies cultivate relationships carefully and slowly so that, eventually, both partners can act and respond instantly.

Partnership, collaboration, and risk-sharing are not new ideas in corporate America. Today's elite companies achieved their success in no small measure by acting on these concepts. However, Instant Involvement companies expand these concepts to a global level, with the intent of improving the value for *all* customers in the entire supply chain, not just for the immediate customer. Instant Involvement companies seek not only to understand the customer and the customer's customer, they help suppliers help them. In short, Instant Involvement companies strive to be the best supplier to their customers *and* the best customer to their suppliers.

In the rocky world of digital commerce, concepts like trust and commitment have become foreign, as both customers and suppliers react and respond to markets conditions that never stop changing. Customers are ever on the lookout for the best value for their money, and so are easily persuaded to switch their loyalties. Companies, out of desperation for survival, make the best choices they can with their limited vision.

Instant Involvement companies strive to be
the best supplier to their customer and the best
customer to their suppliers.

In such a turbulent world, Instant Involvement companies formulate a tightly connected, yet flexible, ecosystem consisting of customers, suppliers, and complementors. This ecosystem is a stable environment in which Instant Involvement companies can let go of fear of betrayal and misaligned loyalties. Only in such an environment can companies stop frantically reacting to every change, actually see the terrain that lies ahead, and take the preparatory actions needed to succeed in the future. Companies that want to thrive in the digital age will have to form ecosystems of their own. They will need to master the discipline of Instant Involvement.

Cisco Systems' Extended Enterprise: An Instant Involvement Company

AS ONE OF THE FASTEST-GROWING COMPANIES IN THE NEW BUSI-
ness world, Cisco Systems makes the data-networking equipment that powers the World Wide Web. Based in Northern
California, over the past 14 years, Cisco has exploded from
start-up status to a $100 billion company. Ninety-five percent

The authors wish to thank Cisco management for their contributions to
this case. We appreciate the input from Tom Fallon and Bob Spiegel, who
helped make sure we had a clear understanding of the Extended Enterprise concept.

of the orders Cisco receives are build-to-order. Cisco works closely with partner suppliers, outsourcing 55 percent of its product fulfillment to supply partners, which bypass the Cisco organization and ship products directly to customers. Ninety-seven percent of orders ship on the date promised, and more than 75 percent of Cisco's orders are received online. Cisco has reduced its cycle time on orders from six to eight weeks to one to three weeks. Cisco is a successful Instant Involvement company.

Cisco's core technology is the router, the device that sends information from one computer to another over the Internet. When a computer on one network sends e-mail or other digitized information to a counterpart on another network, the router finds the location of the destination device and delivers the data.

Acting in Zero Time: Instant Involvement

For Cisco, Instant Involvement is more than an idealized concept; it is part of the company's basic philosophy, called Extended Enterprise. Barbara Siverts, Supply Chain Solutions product manager at Cisco, describes:

> *An Extended Enterprise is a company's extended enterprise of customers, suppliers, and other partners that make up a networked fabric of communication and information exchange, using innovative applications of networked technologies to extend processes through the entire supply chain enterprise. The key principle of an Extended Enterprise is that it extends end to end—from a company's customers all the way through its component suppliers. The linkages along this chain are the critical pieces that give an Extended Enterprise its power, enabling real-time movement of communications and information to each participant in this extended enterprise.*[1]

Linkages put in place by Cisco ensure a symbiotic relationship with strategic partners, and Cisco has set up linkages at multiple levels of its value chain. Bob Spiegel, a director in the Information Systems group responsible for supporting lines of business and strategic programs, describes several of these:

> *At one level are product information linkages. We provide timely product information that is required for the suppliers to build product for us. The faster we communicate, the faster we bring product to market. For example, when an engineering change order is approved, all relevant documentation related to that change is automatically put in a ZIP file and sent to suppliers. We have set up a special channel on our extranet and we push this ZIP file to them. At another level, we have transaction linkages, where suppliers actually initiate transactions on our systems. For example, when they complete an assembly, they can run a closeout transaction on our system telling us they completed the work. That closeout initiates an automatic payment system that pays them for their work. And at a third level we have order fulfillment linkages. Many of our orders are sent directly to our strategic suppliers, who ship directly to the customers. Cisco pays for the parts and the work done by the partner, but we trust them to send the correct parts to the customers at the right time. That linkage in itself means we are very closely tied to our subcontractors. We treat these suppliers just like Cisco plants and hold them to the same standards for quality, cost, and service. Tight integration of systems and processes enable this model to work.*

Instant Involvement benefits Cisco and its extended enterprise in multiple ways. First, Cisco senior managers can focus on their core competencies of product design and marketing, rather than spend time building and managing manufacturing facilities. Second, as demand increases, Cisco can ramp up production either by helping existing partners expand or by taking on new partners. The modularity of outsourcing reduces the complexity of expansion to a simple decision of finding appropriate partners, as opposed to investing in new plants and hiring new employees. Third, Cisco's heavy reliance on information systems integrates the supply chain, resulting in an extended enterprise, which appears to customers as a single organization responding rapidly to customer orders.

Inclusion at Cisco is a basic core value.

Cisco has created a well-balanced ecosystem geared to rapidly respond to customer orders. The ecosystem, driven by instant communication over the Internet, allows suppliers to post quotes and forecasts on Cisco's Web site each quarter. Cisco works with its suppliers' suppliers to make sure they can deliver as needed for Cisco. For example, a processor supplier to one of Cisco's board assembly suppliers is also linked into Cisco's information systems to make sure it can anticipate and prepare for Cisco's customer demand. In addition, Cisco's home page provides partners and suppliers with access to Cisco's Connection Online (CCO), the portal for information and collaboration tasks. CCO, implemented in 1995, is Cisco's interactive online configuration, ordering and order-tracking system. CCO has not only provided unprecedented value to customers, who previously struggled to configure and price systems, but has also enhanced the supply chain for Cisco resellers. One reseller, Sprint, experienced significant savings, as described here:

> *Resellers are flocking to CCO because it lets them get their equipment and finish their jobs much more quickly. At Sprint, it used to take 60 days from the*

*signing of a contract to completing a networking proj-
ect. Now, thanks partly to the efficiency of ordering
Cisco equipment online, it takes 35 to 45 days. Sprint
has also been able to cut its ordering-processing staff
from 21 to 6, allowing the other 15 employees to work,
instead of installing networks, a business that has doubled at Sprint since 1996.*[2]

CCO has helped prepare Cisco vendors to instantly integrate their supply chains with Cisco's. Coupled with the entrepreneurial spirit and the slew of acquisitions made over
the past few years, Cisco has made communicating with the
organizations outside their core structure a standard operating procedure. As Cisco partners use Cisco's Internet-based
communications system, their Instant Involvement with Cisco
becomes a normal part of daily business.

Cisco has created a complete ecosystem geared
to rapid response of customer orders.

New Perspective: Build an Ecosystem

Cisco's ultimate plan, designed by its senior executives, is "to
become lead architect of a brave new infrastructure in which
traditional voice communications and even cable television
networks are subsumed by the Internet."[3] The plan has four
elements:

1. Make Cisco a one-stop shop for wired businesses by assembling a broad product line.
2. Make acquisitions a standard business process.
3. Define industrywide software standards for networking.
4. Pick the right strategic partners.

Early in Cisco's history, executives chose the strategy of acquiring small start-ups with hot technologies and savvy engineers as a means to quickly become a full-service provider. "We figured that if we got engineering talent onboard and helped them finish their products, then let our sales organization and distribution partners market them, we could build new businesses quickly," says Cisco CEO John Chambers. "The trick was to convince these entrepreneurs that they could make a bigger splash with us than they could on their own."[4] By 1999, for every Cisco manufacturing employee, there were six "virtual" employees located around the world who used Cisco processes and were measured against Cisco metrics.

Primary to its success has been the company's
development of instant involvement,
mutual commitment, and strategic partnerships
with a broad yet deep pool of suppliers.

Cisco's savvy strategies, plus its focus on Instant Inclusion, has launched it to the forefront of the networking marketplace. Primary to its success has been the company's development of Instant Involvement, mutual commitment, and strategic partnerships with a broad yet deep pool of suppliers.

Preparatory Action:
Build Mutual Commitment

At Cisco, not every vendor decision is based solely on price. The company has a corporate philosophy of ensuring that suppliers stay profitable and, thus, in business. To implement this philosophy, Cisco shares a wide variety of inventory and demand information with suppliers to help them reduce inventories and operate in Zero Time. In addition, Cisco always pays suppliers within days, rather than weeks, which enables suppliers to reduce the costs of collecting on accounts, thereby gaining more control over their own cash flows. Cisco even involves partners early in the product design process to ensure that products can be manufactured and that parts are available.

Mutual commitment to Cisco also
means mutual investments.

This story illustrates mutual commitment at work at Cisco:

At one point in an interview with Fortune, *Chambers excused himself from a Cisco conference room to make a previously scheduled telephone call. When he returned after a few minutes, he explained: "That was Bill Gates. I wanted to give him a sales lead I got from one of our partners. This wasn't just any old sales lead, by the way. It could mean a lot of business. That's what I mean about being a good partner. Who knows, maybe he'll do the same for me sometime."*[5]

Mutual commitment at Cisco also means mutual investments. Like most companies that have mastered Instant Involvement, Cisco understands that its stringent requirements for partnering can place a heavy burden on supply partners. Cisco carries its portion of the burden by investing in technology and infrastructure that supports both Cisco and its partners. Cisco calls it the Global Networked Business Model, and uses it to manage the supply chain activities that integrate Cisco with its suppliers. Five initiatives summarize the dimensions of that integration:[6]

1. *Single enterprise.* Cisco uses networked applications to integrate suppliers into its production system. Key suppliers are able to operate major portions of the supply chain and to respond instantly to customer demand. The electronic links have eliminated the need for purchase orders and invoice processing.

2. *New product introduction.* Cisco has automated the process for gathering product data, which is used to design prototypes of new products. The automation has reduced the length of the process from one day to 15 minutes, and has resulted in tighter communications between suppliers and Cisco engineers.

3. *Autotest.* Cisco has built test cells that automatically run standardized tests with minimal, if any, labor. Cisco licenses this technology to suppliers, which use it to isolate and correct defects before they reach Cisco.

4. *Direct fulfillment.* Cisco and its suppliers ship orders to customers directly from the location of production. Shipments from suppliers are coordinated with shipments from Cisco to arrive at customer sites simultaneously.

5. *Dynamic replenishment.* Contract manufacturers are able to track Cisco's inventory levels in real time and receive demand information directly from Cisco. Cisco does not filter or alter its information in any way, but sends it instantaneously to suppliers so they can manage their part of the supply chain with accurate data.

To make sure partners use and benefit from the Global Networked Business Model, Cisco expends significant resources to set up and train partners. Its enterprise system is Oracle Applications, and Cisco builds the custom linkages needed to connect to supplier systems. Spiegel describes some of Cisco's activities in this area:

Initially, we created a secure way for suppliers to transact on our ERP system and let our subcontractors have access. We put in the network needed to connect them, and we did all the work on their premises to get them connected. We train them on how to use the systems and on how to do all the transactions they need to do. And since each location of a strategic supplier is unique, we spend a lot of time out at their site answering questions and helping make the implementation smooth. For example, we brought up a supplier in Europe using this model. At that site, the nine-hour time difference made our support model much more complex, causing unique problems.

At Cisco, mutual commitment goes further. For example, with partner Solectron, the tools and organizations are so deeply integrated it is often difficult to tell at which organization an employee works. Cisco links people, processes, tools, and strategies with partners. "If we were to try to disengage from Solectron, it would take years to do so," Tom Fallon, VP of Manufacturing, and a nine-year Cisco veteran, explains. "We would have a very difficult time replacing the capability they give us, and we would find it extremely unpleasant."

"If we were to try to disengage from Solectron,
it would take a year or so to do so."
—T. Fallon, Cisco Manager

Helping its suppliers' suppliers is also important to Cisco. The suppliers of the strategic partners are also included in the information flow. For example, Motorola supplies chips to Solectron for inclusion on boards manufactured for Cisco. Solectron has developed a close relationship with Motorola, whereby they share information about Solectron's needs for Motorola products, some of which ultimately go to Cisco. But Cisco also communicates with Motorola, sending that company a demand profile of what Cisco intends to order from Solectron that will require Motorola processors. In this way, Motorola stays informed and is able to help Solectron help Cisco.

Cisco's deep investment in infrastructure to support its suppliers demonstrates a significant willingness to assume joint risk with suppliers. Cisco, like all Instant Involvement companies, takes the long view on partnerships, and thus invests considerable time and resources to nurture the development of fruitful relationships.

Preparatory Action: Forge Strategic Partnerships

To make the Extended Enterprise philosophy a success, Cisco first had to examine its own capabilities before it could choose the appropriate organizations with which to partner. This is especially true because Cisco outsources most of its manufacturing to supply partners. Cisco's partner selection

---

"We make a commitment to them. If they fail, we fail."
—*T. Fallon*

---

process is based on finding partners with similar philosophies and complementary skills to Cisco, as described in a recent case study:

> *The supply chain functions were jointly performed by Cisco and its contract manufacturers, requiring them to exchange information and interact through labor-intensive processes. As the company began implementing applications to extend to its suppliers and customers, Cisco decided that its core competencies were in design and fulfillment processes rather than in physical*

transformation of product. As a result, Cisco chose to form partnerships with suppliers that performed physical transformation as their core competency. Central to Cisco's philosophy was to remove business barriers that would impede the flow of information within the company and its business partners, further increasing the integration with its constituents and overall power of the supply chain.[7]

Cisco's careful analysis of its own capabilities led naturally to the selection of appropriate strategic partners, which filled the gaps in Cisco's competencies. These partners are part of the Extended Enterprise and are considered an external factory to Cisco. The 20 to 25 strategic partners are linked by more than shared forecasting information. Cisco has built tools that help the suppliers actually run their factories. For example, one initiative is called *dynamic replenishment.* A set of tools that links forecasting, inventory, and backlogs helps the suppliers forecast what they should build, as well as manage how the cycle time will be affected. Cisco complements these tools with meetings with suppliers, during which they discuss and define parameters for success that both partners will use, such as on-time shipments and supplier inventory turns. Fallon explains:

We give our strategic partners data and tools, and sit down with them to agree on what win-win is like. That helps them drive their factories. We don't run their businesses for them. We just give them as many tools as we can to help them help us. For example, Solectron is a strategic supplier for Cisco. We have direct fulfillment with them, where we often pass along an order directly from a customer to Solectron and they send the product directly to the customer. They use our dynamic replenishment tools. Their factories use our autotest monitoring tools to insure our quality standards are met. Overall, we have developed a process architecture to help our suppliers run their factories in a very different way, and our strategic suppliers have openly embraced this approach.

To distribute products, Cisco relies on a variety of organizations, including distributors, consultants, computer-system integrators and manufacturers, and a few telecommunications equipment vendors. Chambers describes this strategy: "Partnering is our heritage. Very few people in this industry partner well, so it's a huge competitive advantage."[8] While Cisco has perhaps more partners than its competitors, the company does not sacrifice quality for volume. Cisco's partnerships have four key characteristics:

1. Maintain the same overall vision of industry trends and direction. Cisco and its partners agree on the potential for network commerce and high-quality multimedia over the Internet.
2. See short-term benefits in terms of real sales from the relationship.
3. See long-term advantages.
4. Share similar values; be aggressive, technologically strong, and known for a focus on customers.

Fallon elaborates on how the partnerships are forged:

We have a Global Supplier Management Group, and they run Commodity Teams, which include buyers from the plants. We look for companies that are large enough to be able to help us and grow with us. They have to have the technical capability we need and [have to] offer us products at a competitive cost. But probably most important is that they have to match our culture. Our business drivers are customer satisfaction and market share gains. We pursue both at all costs. Our partners need to have the same drivers. If instead they were driven on something else, like inventory turns, they would be incompatible with us. We seek partners who pursue the same goals we do.

Cisco supports its partners in multiple ways. First, it single sources from value-added suppliers. The businesses of Cisco and its suppliers are so closely linked that suppliers understand Cisco's dependency on supplier success. Second, the suppliers have individuals involved with key meetings at Cisco, such as design meetings and daily production meetings. For example, Solectron co-locates individuals within Cisco who participate and take responsibility for designing products that are cost-effective to manufacture, make commitments at production meetings for availability of material, and drive process improvements for asset goals. Fallon summarizes this by saying, "We made a commitment to them. If they fail, we fail."

Cisco also takes risks with its partners. Cisco pays for all parts needed by supplier partners and pays immediately for completed assemblies. For example, Cisco has suppliers close out transactions and initiate payment without involvement from any Cisco employees. Spiegel explains:

We were looking for ways to help our subcontractors reduce cost, and learned that cash flow was a big issue. They have to tie up a lot of money in inventory for Cisco, and they passed that cost on to us. So we changed that. First, we identify strategic (usually expensive) parts, and utilize the Cisco ERP system to have Cisco financially own these yet physically store them at the supplier. Second, as soon as the assembly is completed, we have the supplier perform a completion transaction that initiates immediate payment. Cisco then carries these completed assemblies in inventory at the supplier's location. This shortens the cash cycle and reduces cost.

Once partnerships have been established, Cisco freely gives and seeks advice from partners on standard operating procedures:

As he does most days, Chambers spends nearly half his time with customers, pitching woo and asking for report cards. He has breakfast with Sun's McNealy, at which he forgets to eat breakfast, and a lunch meeting with the information technology department of Bankers Trust, at which he eats no lunch. He receives a primer on contemporary Japanese politics from renowned McKinsey consultant Kenichi Ohmae, and jokes with fellow West Virginians who happen by in a delegation from WorldCom. [9]

Not every supplier is a strategic partner at Cisco. Cisco actually works with two different types of suppliers. There are strategic partners, like Solectron, which are significant value-added suppliers. But other suppliers, called preferred manufacturers, are used for commodity parts. Fallon explains:

Preferred manufacturers supply commodity parts, like resistors. We typically have several suppliers for those types of parts, and all must meet our basic level of quality, availability, and price. We share our forecasts with them so they can plan their capacities. But we do not get as involved with them as we do with our strategic partners.

How Cisco Makes It Work

Cisco has set up a series of business processes that help its suppliers help Cisco, beginning with a culture of sharing information and integrating physical and staff capabilities as much as possible. Fallon described a key perspective at Cisco when he differentiated between shared and nonshared data:

When thinking about sharing information with suppliers, some companies start with the perspective of deciding what information they can share. They start with a blank piece of paper and list data they think will be reasonable to share. It gives them a certain perspective on what information they are then able to share with customers, suppliers, and everyone. We take a different perspective from the beginning. We start with the assumption that everything can be shared, and then we pull out what we really don't want shared. It forces us to identify key important bits of information that are really not necessary to the collaboration. And we end up with an entirely different list than if we started the other way.

Inclusion at Cisco is a basic core value. The company has built an intranet that makes it possible for employees around the world to interact and complete most business processes. For example, salespeople can do all of their tasks on the intranet, from learning about new products to checking availability and delivery schedules, to placing orders and tracking them. Even most of the human resource tasks can be done over the Web, including activities like checking benefits and updating personnel information. By one estimate, more than 1.7 million pages of information are available to employees. The network, the Cisco Employee Connection (CEC), streamlines business processes for employees, which in turn lowers the cost of doing the necessary administrative tasks. Further, just about every application in the company uses Web browsers as their only user interface.

As Cisco partners use Cisco's Internet-based communication system, their instant involvement with Cisco becomes a normal part of daily business.

Inclusion of individual employees, even when they are traveling, is important at Cisco. Distance learning and communication are standard operating methods for Cisco. Learning modules are accessible from employee's desktop at the office, at home, and on the road. More important, Internet-based communication is frequently used. For example, when CEO Chambers addressed employees at Cisco's quarterly meeting in late 1997, the number of employees who were able to see and hear Chambers was more than double the norm because the meeting was made available over the Internet in real time. About 2,000 employees were able to either view the speech live at their desktops or see a delayed broadcast over the intranet. Thus, Chambers was able to deliver his message directly to a significant number of employees, rather than rely on word of mouth, which often distorts or changes the message.

Practicing the discipline of Instant Involvement is a combination of processes, values, and technologies that enable the right information to flow to the right organization in the right time.

The culture at Cisco is entrepreneurial. With so many acquisitions happening at such a fast pace, the culture there could easily be chaotic. But Chambers and his staff have worked to keep the employees it has inherited from acquisitions. In fact, a measure of success of the acquisition is how many employees stay with Cisco.

The Cisco culture also values listening to and sharing information with employees. Team building is nurtured, and team players are the most popular employees. Stories are told of how Chambers walks around the office handing out ice cream to those in the office and chatting with them about everything from their current projects to ideas about improving the workplace.

In sum, Cisco combines a unique perspective for inclusion in all internal and external activities. Practicing the discipline of Instant Involvement is a combination of processes, values, and technologies that enable the right information to flow to the right organization at the right time. Cisco has clearly mastered this combination.

Messages for Managers

The Cisco case highlights several important lessons about becoming an Instant Involvement company.

- *Picking the right strategic partners is critical to the success of both your company and your partner's company.* Cisco is selective about partners because it relies on these partners to complement the company's core business. Cisco partners join the company in both risk and reward, confident that their strong relationship will guarantee success.

"We take a different perspective. We start with the assumption that everything can be shared, and then we pull out what we really don't want shared."

—T. Fallon

- *Enabling instant response, which is possible only if partners throughout the value chain of your company can become instantly involved.* When partners are carefully selected, trust and open communication become part of the shared culture as at Cisco. Cisco is thus able to share the links of its value chain that other companies would never consider sharing. Cisco has built information systems that make instant communications, and hence Instant Involvement, possible.

- *Trusting your partners is the only way to build a strategic partnership.* Trust is necessary in order to share more than inventory levels. At Cisco, trust is established by acquiring some companies and keeping their employees; by seeking ways to constantly improve the work life and environment of both acquired employees and Cisco employees; and by sharing that value with partners. Also, helping its suppliers help Cisco means trusting them enough to involve vendors in new market directions, customer acquisition and retention, and possibly even in improving Cisco's organizational structure itself.

- *Believing in a win-win philosophy to build long-term relationships.* Supporting your partners when they need it is the quickest way to help your own organization. Abandoning your strategic partner in time of need shakes the foundation of all your partners. Cisco has made it a requirement to help its suppliers. In some cases, it means acquiring them in order to help them sustain their employment; in other cases, it means helping them design systems that interface with Cisco so they can better integrate their information systems.

CHAPTER

It's about Time

WE HAVE DESCRIBED HOW THE NEW LEADERS OF THE DIGITAL ERA can use the five Zero Time disciplines to find the *white space,* accumulate *lead time,* and achieve market *lock-in.* We've shown you how the more traditional leaders of the business world—giants like IBM and GE—were compelled to let go of much of their knowledge and traditional functions to survive in today's marketplace. And we've written about how the dot.coms and start-ups have organized to take customer share away from the traditional market leaders. We've condensed the lessons learned by these elite companies, dot.coms, and start-ups into guidelines for mastering the Zero Time disciplines. We call them the Ten Commandments of Zero Time Organizations (Table 13.1):

1. *Thou shall always live in Zero Time.* Infuse the goal of acting instantly into your culture. Zero Time is not about speeding up the business, it's about designing for speed from the beginning. Every component of the organization is challenged to continuously adapt, to

Table 13.1   The Ten Commandments of Zero Time

1. Thou shall always live in Zero Time.
2. Thou shall look for white space.
3. Thou shall accumulate lead time.
4. Thou shall use the T-Strategy in every new market.
5. Thou shall honor your customer and your customer's customer.
6. Thou shall build instantly executable processes.
7. Thou shall not kill your employee's drive and enthusiasm.
8. Thou shall build learning into every task.
9. Thou shall not abandon your supplier.
10. Thou shall listen and communicate.

ensure they are able to respond instantly to requests, issues, and opportunities. In short, living in Zero Time
means organizing to provide instant CUSTOMERization.

2. *Thou shall look for the white space.* Identify the white
   space. It is where your customers are going and from
   where new customers are coming. Zero Time organizations look for those opportunities to anticipate what
   the customers will want and to be the first to satisfy
   those needs. The white space is not what customers
   want today, but what they want tomorrow. The Zero
   Time company is perfectly positioned to anticipate and
   deliver.

3. *Thou shall accumulate lead time.* Anticipate where
   and when you need to invest in core competencies.
   The Zero Time organization leverages its core competencies into market after market. That means building
   in capabilities to respond *before* they are needed.

4. *Thou shall use the T-Strategy in every new market.*
   Evolve strategically to achieve perpetual market lock-
   in. Like zero defects, Zero Time is about thinking differently from the beginning. The goal is perpetual
   market lock-in, not just temporary market dominance.

Keeping a narrow focus on the core competency is critical to successfully leveraging advantages from the Zero Time framework.

5. *Thou shall honor your customer and your customer's customer.* Align the values of your organization with those of your customer. Zero Time companies know what drives their customers. It is *their* customer. Get to know what their customers are demanding of them, and you will honor your customer; and they will honor you in return.

6. *Thou shall build instantly executable processes.* Design your business processes to make them instantly executable. Operational processes, support processes, and even management processes are all candidates not just for automation, but for transformation, as they are reexamined and redesigned to be instantaneous.

7. *Thou shall not kill drive and enthusiasm.* Establish a culture, structure, and environment where every individual, group, and team is empowered and enabled. That means empowering workers, as well as building systems that guide workers to align their actions with corporate goals, so that they are able to do what is required of them.

8. *Thou shall build learning into every task.* Make a commitment to instant learning. Zero Time organizations do not separate learning and knowledge management. Instead, they build comprehensive learning strategies that utilize knowledge management systems and seamlessly integrate them into the business processes. The delivery of knowledge is instantly available to whomever needs it in order to create customer value and loyalty.

9. *Thou shall not abandon your supplier.* Treat your suppliers and vendors as you want your customers to treat you. Zero Time companies partner with key suppliers, and share information, ideas, and technology in

order to help the suppliers help them. They select strategic partners, then treat those partners as extensions of the Zero Time organization.

10. *Thou shall listen and communicate.* Build a culture and infrastructure that enables and supports communications among workers and between your business and your customers and suppliers. Communication does not mean telling all to everyone; it means making information available and accessible in an easy manner. More important, it means listening. Listening to customers tell you how to align your business strategy. Listening to suppliers tells you how to help them help you. Listening to your employees tells you how to help them help your customers.

We have written about time: Zero Time. We have shown how Zero Time molds and shapes a firm's CUSTOMERization processes. Zero Time is organizing for instant CUSTOMERization. Zero Time provides instant customer value. Every time. All the time.

NOTES

INTRODUCTION

1. G. Stalk Jr. and T. Hout. 1990. *Competing against Time.* New York, NY: McGraw-Hill.

2. K.M. Eisenhardt and S.L. Brown, "Time Pacing: Competing in Markets That Won't Stand Still." *Harvard Business Review,* vol. 76(2), March–April 1998, pp. 59-69.

3. S. Kirsner. "Laurie A. Tucker." *Fast Company,* December 1999, pp. 166-172.

4. G. Imperato. "Book Report—Time Keeps Getting Faster." *Net Company (Fast Company* supplement), Fall 1999, p. 7.

CHAPTER 1

1. D.J. Boorstin. 1974. *The Americans: The Democratic Experience.* New York: Vintage Books.

2. C. Hartman and R. Rodin. 1999. *Free, Perfect, and Now: Connecting to the Three Insatiable Customer Demands: A CEO's True Story.* New York: Simon & Schuster.

3. "Fast Company." Fast Company poll. May, 2000. www .fastcompany.com/cgi-bin/votato/in.cg?zerotime_r.

CHAPTER 2

1. A. Morita, with E. Reingold and M. Shimomura. 1986. *Made in Japan: Akio Morita and Sony.* New York: Dutton.

2. J. Nathan. 1999. *SONY—The Private Life.* Boston, MA: Houghton Mifflin Company.

3. Ibid.

4. A. Yu. 1998. *Creating the Digital Future.* New York: The Free Press.

5. C. Handy. 1994. *The Age of Paradox.* Cambridge, MA: Harvard Business School Press.

6. M. Treacy and F. Wiersema. 1995. *Discipline of Market Leaders.* Reading, MA: Addison-Wesley.

7. G. Moore. 1995. *Inside the Tornado.* New York: Harper-Collins.

8. W. Zellner and S. Anderson Forest, with D. Morris and L. Lee, "The Big Guys Go Online," *BusinessWeek,* September 6, 1999, pp. 30-31.

CHAPTER 3

1. P. Seybold. 1999. *Customers.com.* New York: Times Books.

2. S. Greco. December 1998. "Choose or Lose." *Inc.,* pp. 57-66.

3. R.T. Yeh. 1999. *Singapore's Economic Development Board as a Near Zero Time Company.* Austin, TX: University of Texas at Austin, ICC Institute.

4. K. Pearlson and R. Yeh. 1999. *Dell Computers as a Near Zero Time Company.* Austin, TX: University of Texas at Austin, ICC Institute.

5. A. Yu. 1998. *Creating the Digital Future.* New York: The Free Press.

6. Pearlson and Yeh, *Dell Computers.*

7. Greco, "Choose or Lose."

8. Seybold, *Customers.com.*

9. D. Pepper and M. Rogers. 1998. *The One to One Future.* New York: Doubleday.

10. S. Kirsner. June 1999. "DOROTHY LANE Loves Its Customers." *Fast Company,* pp. 76-78.

11. Yeh, *Singapore's Economic Development Board.*

12. Pearlson and Yeh, *Dell Computers.*

13. Seybold, *Customers.com.*

14. C. Handy. 1994. *The Age of Paradox.* Boston, MA: Harvard Business School Press.

CHAPTER 4

1. D. Tapscott. 1996. *Digital Economy*. New York: McGraw Hill.

2. S. Kirsner. "Laurie A. Tucker." *Fast Company*, December 1999, pp. 166–172.

3. Ibid.

4. P. Seybold. 1999. *Customers.com*. New York: Times Books.

5. D. Paul and K. Pearlson. August 1995. *Federal Express: The Role of Information Technology in Customer Service*. Austin, TX: University of Texas Graduate School of Business.

6. Tapscott, *Digital Economy*.

CHAPTER 5

1. S. Goldman, R. Nagel, and K. Priess. 1995. *Agile Competitors and Virtual Organizations*. New York: Van Nostrand Reinhold Publishers.

2. K. Pearlson and R. Yeh. 1999. *Dell Computers as a Near Zero Time Company*. Austin, TX: University of Texas at Austin, IC² Institute.

3. Dell Learning. Summer 1999. "A Perspective on How We Work," internal document. Austin, TX: Dell Computer Corporation, p. 3.

4. As cited in C. Dahle. December 1998. "Learning: Our Challenge Is to Put the Learner in Charge of the Process: John Coné." *Fast Company*, p. 180.

5. T. Davenport and L. Prusak. 1998. *Working Knowledge*. Boston: HBS Press.

6. Ibid.

7. I. Nonaka and H. Takeuchi. 1995. *The Knowledge-Creating Company*. New York: Oxford University Press.

8. B. Gates. 1999. *Business @ the Speed of Thought*. New York: Warner Books.

9. J. O'Neil, K. Ostrofsky, and J.I. Cash. *Otis Elevator: Managing the Service Force*. Case Study 9-191-213, Boston, MA: Harvard Business School, Division of Research.

10. P. Senge. 1990. *The Fifth Discipline*. New York: Doubleday Currency.

11. "Motorola." August 15, 1999. www.motorola.com. And Motorola. 1994. Annual Report. Austin, TX: Motorola Corporation.

12. Imperato, "Learning without Limits."

CHAPTER 6

1. C. Dahle. December 1998. "Learning: Our Challenge Is to Put the Learner in Charge of the Process: John Coné." *Fast Company,* p. 180.

2. Ibid.

3. "Dell Computer Corporation." July 20, 1999. www.dell.com.

4. Dahle, *Fast Company.*

CHAPTER 7

1. J.R. Katzenback and D.K. Smith. 1994. *The Wisdom of Teams.* Boston, MA: Harvard Business School Press.

2. J.C. Collins and J.I. Porras. 1994. *Build to Last.* New York: HarperCollins Publishers, Inc.

3. W.E. Deming. 1992. *Out of the Crisis.* Cambridge, MA: Center for Advanced Engineering Study, MIT.

4. F.J. Aguilar and A. Bhambri. 1984. "Johnson & Johnson (A)," Boston, MA: Harvard Business School Press. Case No. 384-053, p. 4.

5. S.J. Boorstin. 1974. *The Americans: The Democratic Experience.* New York: Vintage Books.

6. P. Senge. 1990. *The Fifth Discipline.* New York: Doubleday.

7. G. Hamel and C.K. Prahalad. 1994. *Competing for the Future,* Boston, MA: Harvard Business School Press.

8. Ibid.

9. T.J. Watson Jr. 1990. *Father Son & Co.* New York: Bantam Books.

10. G. Bethune, with S. Huler. 1998. *From Worst to First.* New York: John Wiley & Sons, Inc.

11. D. Petersen and J. Hillkiak. 1991. *A Better Idea.* Boston, MA: Houghton Mifflin Co.

12. A. Yu. 1998. *Creating the Digital Future.* New York: The Free Press.

13. P. Riley. 1993. *The Winner Within.* New York: Berkeley Books.

14. F. Ostroff. 1999. *The Horizontal Organization.* New York: Oxford University Press.

15. S.R. Covey. 1992. *Principle-Centered Leadership.* New York: Simon & Schuster.

CHAPTER 8

1. N. Tichy and S. Stratford. 1999. *Control Your Destiny or Someone Else Will.* New York: Doubleday.

2. R. Slater. 1999. *Jack Welch and the GE Way.* New York: McGraw-Hill, Inc.

3. September 18, 1999. "General Electric: The House That Jack Built." *The Economist,* pp. 23–26.

4. Tichy and Stratford. *Control Your Destiny.*

5. Slater. *Jack Welch and the G.E. Way.*

6. R. Pascale. 1990. *Managing on the Edge.* New York: Simon & Schuster.

7. C.A. Barlett and M. Wozny. July 28, 1999. *GE's Two-Decade Transformation: Jack Welch's Leadership.* Case Study 9–399-150, Boston, MA: Harvard Business School.

8. J.L. Heskett. March 16, 1999. *GE . . . We Bring Good Things to Life. (A)* Case Study 9–899-162, Boston, MA: Harvard Business School.

9. Barlett and Wozny, *GE's Two-Decade Transformation.*

10. Ibid.

11. John F. Welch. "Today's Leaders Look to Tomorrow," *Fortune,* March 26, 1990.

12. Tichy and Strafford, *Control Your Destiny.*

13. Q. Slater. *Jack Welch and the GE Way.*

14. J.A. Byren. June 1998. "How Jack Welch Runs GE: A Special Report," *BusinessWeek,* pp. 92–111.

15. Ibid.

16. J. Lowe. 1998. *Jack Welch Speaks.* New York: John Wiley & Sons, Inc.

17. Slater. *Jack Welch and the GE Way.*

18. Ibid.

19. "General Electric: The House that Jack Built."

20. Tichy and Stratford. *Control Your Destiny.*

21. Barlett and Wozny. *GE's Two-Decade Transformation.*

CHAPTER 9

1. M. Hammer and J. Champy. 1993. *Reengineering the Corporation.* HarperBusiness.

2. See B. Tedeshci. April 19, 1999. "The Net's Real Business Happens .Com to .Com; A Market That Dwarfs Retail E-Sales." *The New York Times,* p. 1B.

3. P. Rosenzweig. 1994. *International Sourcing in Athletic Footware: Nike and Reebok.* Case Study 394–189, Boston, MA: HBS Publishing.

4. S. Goldman, R. Nagel, and K. Preiss. 1995. *Agile Competitors and Virtual Organizations.* New York: Van Nostrand Reinhold Publishers, p. 5.

5. Ibid.

6. K. Priess. "A Systems Perspective of Lean and Agile Manufacturing." *Agility and Global Competition Journal,* Winter 1997, vol. 1, no. 1, pp. 59–76.

7. Goldman et al. *Agile Competitors,* p. 16.

8. Adapted from ibid.

9. J.R. Caron, S.L. Jarvenpaa, and D.B. Stoddard. September 1994. "Business Reengineering at CIGNA Corporation: Experiences and Lessons Learned from the First Five Years." *MIS Quarterly,* vol. 18, no. 3.

10. Adapted from M. Hammer. July 1992. "Don't Automate, Obliterate." *Harvard Business Review,* Article 90406.

11. Adapted from the Otisline Case Study Series. W. McFarlan and D. Stoddard. July 1990. *Otisline (A).* Case Study 186304, Boston, MA: Harvard Business School, Division of Research. And J. O'Neil, K. Ostrofsky, and J.L. Cash. June 1991. "Otis Elevator: Managing the Service Force." Case Study 191213, Boston, MA: Harvard Business School, Division of Research.

CHAPTER 10

1. Progressive Insurance Company. 1998. Annual Report. Cleveland, OH: Progressive Insurance Company.

2. Ibid.

3. C. Salter. November 1998. "Progressive Makes Big Claims." *Fast Company.*

4. M. Hammer and J. Champy. 1993. *Reengeering the Corporation.* HarperBusiness.

5. C. Salter. "Progressive Makes Big Claims."

6. Progressive Insurance Company, Annual Report.

7. "Progressive Insurance Company," September 28, 1999, www.progressive.com.

8. C. Salter. "Progressive Makes Big Claims."

9. Ibid.

10. Progressive Insurance Company, Annual Report.

CHAPTER 11

1. June 26, 1999. "Business and the Internet: The Net Imperative." *Economist Special Section,* pp. 5–40.

2. Ibid.

3. S. Signorelli and J. Heskett. February 1989. *Benetton (A),* Case Study 685-014, Boston, MA: Harvard Business School.

4. "Business and the Internet."

5. Adapted from B. Tedeshci. April 19, 1999. "The Net's Real Business Happens .Com to .Com: A Market That Dwarfs Retail E-Sales." *The New York Times,* p. 1B.

6. A. Yu. 1998. *Creating the Digital Future.* New York: Free Press.

7. "Wal-Mart." September 15, 1999. www.walmart.com.

8. "PETsMART," September 15, 1999. www.petsmart.com and "IBM," September 15, 1999. www.ibm.com.

9. PETsMART Annual Report from form 10k (file # 0-21888) filed with the SEC on April 26, 1999.

10. "Wal-Mart," September 15, 1999. www.walmart.com.

11. M. Bensaou. Summer 1999. "Portfolios of Buyer-Supplier Relationships." *Sloan Management Review,* pp. 35–44.

12. "IBM," September 15, 1999. www.ibm.com.

CHAPTER 12

Much of the material in this chapter was adapted from these publications:

R. Austin, R. Nolan, and M. Cotteleer. October 1999. "Cisco Systems, Inc: Implementing ERP." Case Study 699-022, Boston, MA: Harvard Business School.

Cisco Annual Reports for 1997 and 1998.

H. Green. July 26, 1999. "The Information Gold Mine." *BusinessWeek,* e.biz, p. EB17.

R. Nolan and K. Porter. October 13, 1998. "Cisco Systems, Inc." Case Study 9-398-127, Boston, MA: Harvard Business School.

B. Schlender. May 12, 1997. "Computing's Next Superpower." *Fortune,* 135(9), pp. 88-101.

1. B. Siverts. "Cisco's Extended Enterprise Delivers Competitive Advantage," White Paper, www.siverts.ascet.com.

2. S. Tully. August 17, 1998. "How Cisco Mastered the Net." *Fortune,* 138(4), pp. 207-210.

3. B. Schlender. May 12, 1997. "Computing's Next Superpower." *Fortune,* 135(9), pp. 88-101.

4. Ibid.

5. Ibid.

6. R. Nolan and K. Porter. October 13, 1998. "Cisco Systems, Inc." Case Study 9-398-127, Boston, MA: Harvard Business School.

7. Ibid.

8. Schendler. "Computing's Next Superpower."

9. A. Kupfer. September 7, 1998. "The Real King of the Internet." *Fortune,* 138(5), pp. 84-93.

INDEX

265